Just Keep Digging
By Rodney Burton

Just Keep Digging
Copyright © 2013
Rodney Burton

Published by CreateSpace Independent Publishing Platform.

This title is also available as an eBook. Visit
www.amazon.com

Contributor: Rodney Burton
Editors: Kim Burton, Debbie Nelson, LaDonna Nolden, Mary Ann Powell.
Cover design: Rodney Burton
Cover Artwork: Layout design courtesy of CreateSpace.
Image courtesy of Photography by BJWOK at
FreeDigitalPhotos.net
First Printing 2013
Printed in the United States of America

ISBN-13: 978-1490394619
ISBN-10: 1490394613

All Bible verses are the "New American Standard" version of the Bible unless otherwise noted.

Dedication

To my wonderful Lord and Savior, Jesus Christ, Who is not only the inspiration for this book, but the inspiration for my life.

To my wonderful and loving wife, Kim, who gives me the strength, courage, and encouragement to keep going, no matter how difficult things may seem or become.

To my wonderful son, Josiah, who inspires me daily. My prayer is that he would always know that all of his dreams can become a reality if he trusts God and applies what God has given to him.

To the people we have served in our ministry assignments in Indiana, Missouri and Kentucky.

To the people of Calvary Church in Carthage, Illinois, where my family and I have the privilege of serving as pastors. As we continue to dig for and pursue God's best, I am reminded how blessed we are to have such a wonderful group of people on the journey with us.

About the Author

Rodney Burton, along with his wife Kim and son Josiah, currently serve as lead pastors of Calvary Church in Carthage, Illinois. Rodney and Kim are graduates of the Brownsville Revival School of Ministry in Pensacola, Florida. Rodney is ordained with the Assemblies of God. Their heart is to see the church come alive with the power, presence and fullness of God. They feel the church has been living far below her potential and is in great need of a mighty move of God. Rodney's preaching and writing is built around and driven by this passionate belief. You can learn more about the Burtons by visiting www.rodneyburton.net or their church website www.calvarychurchag.com.

Rodney's other published works:

"31 Keys to Possessing Your Promise"

"Carrying the Torch for Revival" (with Tom Stamman)

Contents

Introduction

The sound of the ram in the thicket must have been a wonderful and welcome sound for Isaac, as he looked up at his father Abraham, who stood with his slaying knife aimed at his son (see Genesis 22). Isaac was the promised son born to Abraham and Sarah, and God had challenged Abraham to offer him as a sacrifice. Isaac got to see first-hand the faith of his father in a way that no one else was able to experience.

It was a part of life for Isaac – seeing the faith of his father Abraham. Isaac lived what the rest of us can only imagine and sing about (remember "Father Abraham?"). He was continuously exposed to the faith and belief in God that made Abraham such an important historical figure. How many times did Isaac hear the story about his miraculous birth? How many of his birthday parties would have included the story of the Lord visiting Abraham to promise a son? What must have been going through Isaac's mind as he and his father were on their way up the mountain to sacrifice on the day God sent a ram in place of Isaac?

I wonder if Isaac ever felt intimidation or insignificance as a result of the example of faith he witnessed in his father. Were there times when Isaac wondered if he would ever know and experience God in the same way as his father? Did Isaac battle with the uncertainty of following his father's lead, of walking in the same faith he grew up around day after day?

In the pages of this book we will explore Isaac's process of seeking to find and discover for himself the God of his father Abraham. Our foundational Scripture for this book is found in Genesis 26:

Then Isaac dug again the wells of water which had been dug in the days of his father Abraham, for the Philistines had stopped them up after the death of Abraham; and he gave them the same names which his father had given them.
Genesis 26:18-19

Isaac was experiencing blessing in his own life, and others around him were recognizing that he was enjoying God's blessing. Abraham had died and Isaac had been given his inheritance; and we find that "*after the death of Abraham, that God blessed his son Isaac; and Isaac lived by Beer-lahai-roi*" *(Genesis 25:11).* Abimelech and others around began to recognize that Isaac was living in God's favor; however, Isaac was trying to find his own way. He was trying to come to the realization that indeed God was there for *him* like He had been for his father Abraham.

So we find that Isaac dug again the wells of his father which had been covered by the Philistines. To cover a well in ancient times was a declaration of war. The nourishment and provision that Abraham had opened and had made available to his family had been eliminated. When Isaac found himself in that same region he felt the need to re-open those wells.

Consider this picture perfect example. Abraham, the father, had opened the wells designed to provide for his family a continual source of nourishment, life and strength. The parallel we can draw is that our Father in Heaven has opened much in the spirit for us to enjoy as a continuous source of nourishment, life and strength. In the same way in which the wells Abraham had dug had been covered over by the enemy, so too has our enemy, the devil, covered over the spiritual sources opened to us by our Father. The intimidating stance the enemy has taken is as if to say, "I have taken away

7

something that was prepared for you by the Father, and I do not think there is anything you can do about it."

Yet, in our story from Genesis 26, we find something inside of Isaac that wanted to reconnect with the wells, with the provision of his father Abraham. Something inside of him wanted to declare that the Philistines – the enemy – could not intimidate or control him. Isaac felt the need to find again the well, the living water that had been discovered by his father, and that was the rightful possession of the people of God.

In the following pages we will explore the journey of discovery experienced by Isaac. From that journey we will consider in our own lives the journey of discovering the provision of God our Father for ourselves.

*He who believes in Me, as the Scripture said, 'From his innermost being will flow rivers of **living water**.'*
John 7:38

The promise is that from within will flow the nourishing, provisional and spiritual waters from God. For some reading this, you can remember how those waters flowed in your father or mother. You can remember a time when you enjoyed those waters, and there is something inside of you that wants to dig and re-discover those waters again today in your own life. Like Isaac, however, the digging and searching for what you remember is not going to be an easy journey. But for the one who continues to the end, you will discover, like Isaac, the blessing and presence of God. And you will discover the beauty of God, making the personal connection in your life that declares He is *your* God and not just the God of those who have gone before you.

So let us embark on this journey together as we just keep digging.

8

Section 1: Valley of Gerar

So Isaac went to Gerar, to Abimelech king of the Philistines. The Lord appeared to him and said, "Do not go down to Egypt; stay in the land of which I shall tell you. Sojourn in this land and I will be with you and bless you, for to you and to your descendants I will give all these lands, and I will establish the oath which I swore to your father Abraham. I will multiply your descendants as the stars of heaven, and will give your descendants all these lands; and by your descendants all the nations of the earth shall be blessed, because Abraham obeyed Me and kept My charge, My commandments, My statutes and My laws." So Isaac lived in Gerar....Now all the wells which his father's servants had dug in the days of Abraham his father, the Philistines stopped up by filling them with earth. Then Abimelech said to Isaac, "Go away from us, for you are too powerful for us." And Isaac departed from there and camped in the valley of Gerar, and settled there.
Genesis 26:1-6, 15-17

The word valley is defined as a narrow place in which a brook runs.

Gerar means a lodging or holding place. It is a sojourning.

Chapter 1: This Valley is Dry

So Isaac lived in Gerar....Now Isaac sowed in that land and reaped in the same year a hundredfold. And the Lord blessed him, and the man became rich, and continued to grow richer until he became very wealthy; for he had possessions of flocks and herds and a great household, so that the Philistines envied him.
Genesis 26:6, 12-14

Gerar is a significant city in the Bible in that it was where both Abraham and Isaac spoke of their wives, Sarah and Rebekah respectively, as being their sister when asked by the Philistines. Both father and son acted in fear that the Philistines would treat them badly in hopes of getting their wives for themselves. In this book, I am not looking to cover the details of that connection with Gerar. Rather, let us consider Isaac's journey of finding the water of promise from God.

It was in Gerar where this journey began. Prior to moving to and living in Gerar, Isaac had been living in Beer-lahai-roi (see Genesis 25:11). This region had been a part of the family for some time, as it was while Isaac was near Beer-lahai-roi when he saw Rebekah coming to meet him and to later become his wife (see Genesis 24:62). The first time this city is mentioned is in Genesis 16, when the Angel of the Lord finds Hagar near the spring or well that became known as Beer-lahai-roi. Hagar had become pregnant by Abraham at the request of Sarah and then things began to go sour. Hagar was running from Abraham and Sarah, but the Lord met her at this well and told her to return and be blessed.

Beer-lahai-roi means "well of the living One seeing me" or "well of the life of vision."[1] Isaac had spent years around this well. Yet, it was the well that was most connected with the attempt by Isaac's parents to produce by natural means the promise of God that he represented. This well represented man's attempt to naturally produce something supernatural. And we find at the beginning of Genesis 26 that there was a famine in the land; therefore Isaac moved on and settled in Gerar.

As mentioned in the introduction to this section, a "valley" is generally defined as a narrow place where a brook would run. However, this reference here in Genesis speaks of a place in need of water. The Valley of Gerar, then, speaks of the low point of the region that was in need of water. Commonly, in the valley a brook would run but that was not the case here. Here, in Gerar, it was dry.

It is often much easier to act deceptively when you find yourself in a dry and barren place. When it seems as though you are reaching, grasping, or hoping, the need to fabricate something can become quite strong. Do you find in your own life that when you are feeling dry, the draw and appeal to act deceptively or in a compromising fashion is stronger? It was in Gerar, the place which represented dryness, where both Abraham and Isaac acted in a deceptive manner in regard to their wives.

How Did I End Up Here?

Did this question linger in Isaac's mind? With everything he had seen and experienced in his life up to this point, how did he end up in Gerar? How did he end up in a dry place? Consider what God had just spoken to Isaac:

---

[1] Blueletterbible.org

The Lord appeared to him and said, "Do not go down to Egypt; stay in the land of which I shall tell you. Sojourn in this land and I will be with you and bless you, for to you and to your descendants I will give all these lands, and I will establish the oath which I swore to your father Abraham. I will multiply your descendants as the stars of heaven, and will give your descendants all these lands; and by your descendants all the nations of the earth shall be blessed; because Abraham obeyed Me and kept My charge, My commandments, My statutes and My laws."
So Isaac lived in Gerar.
Genesis 26:2-6

The Lord appeared to Isaac and spoke to him that he was to not go to Egypt, but to sojourn or stay in this land and enjoy God's presence and blessing. The natural tendency then would be for Isaac to reason that God was about to do great and mighty things in his life. God was keeping Isaac away from Egypt – the proverbial worldly or dry place – and He was going to pour out His blessing. Obviously greater things were about to be realized by Isaac and those with him.

Yet, Isaac lived in Gerar. Does that not seem contradictory? Isaac had a decision to make. He could feel sorry for himself. He could begin to reason that God had given him some misinformation. He could question whether he had even heard from God in the first place. He could start to question God's ability to fulfill what he thought to be God's promise. Or, he could trust God to be faithful and not allow himself to view God through the eyes of the circumstances in which he found himself.

How many times have you felt as though something had derailed you from what you perceived to be God's planned destination? How many of you who are reading these words right now find yourself in Gerar and you cannot seem to figure out what God is doing or why He is choosing to do things in this manner?

I recall a time when I was going through a string of events that seemed contradictory to what I felt God was doing at the time. I became frustrated and shared those feelings with God. He simply reminded me that everything is Father filtered, and I needed to walk through this difficult stretch with the same trust and confidence as I had been walking through the easier time.

So many times we can get caught up in the moment of difficulty or despair and quickly forget that which compelled us to begin the journey in the first place. Throughout Scripture and throughout history, the journey from God's promise to God's provision is not typically a quick and easy jump. Many times the road is marked by speed bumps and potholes. The journey often causes us to define situations as either obstacles or opportunities.

What Do I Do Here?

Isaac could have easily defined Gerar as an obstacle. Instead he saw it as an opportunity. Isaac saw an opportunity to dig deeper and rediscover the God of his father, and to uncover the God he needed in his own life. So many times our journey to the mountaintops with God is defined by our response in the valleys. If we lie down, roll over or quit in the valley then we will never experience the mountain.

The lessons and the growth that are available to us in the valley times are invaluable in preparing us for our journey up the mountain and our time on the mountain. The Song of Solomon describes God in these terms:

I am the rose of Sharon, the lily of the valleys.
Song of Solomon 2:1

Lily bulbs are starchy and edible. In areas in which they are eaten, they are primarily marketed as health food. Lily bulbs are often eaten in summer, for their perceived ability to reduce internal heat.[2] I was complaining one time about the valley experiences in my life and the Lord brought me to this passage. His word to me that day was this: "If you do not go through the valley, how will you ever encounter the Lily of the Valley?"

When Isaac found himself living in Gerar, he responded by digging the wells of his father Abraham. To dig is defined "to break up, turn over or remove usually earth or sand in an attempt to obtain or unearth something beneath."[3] In our passage it means to dig a well in search for water. The implication is that Isaac was digging the wells of his father Abraham searching for what he must have remembered from his past, or that he remembered his father having enjoyed. Isaac was trying to find what had belonged to his father, and what he believed belonged to him as well.

Isaac made a conscious choice to not settle in the valley, but rather to move forward toward realizing what God had promised to him. As we continue on this journey with Isaac, we will explore the journey of discovery that Isaac found himself on as he dug the wells. We will also consider the principles Isaac learned and how we, too, can journey toward discovering all that God has made available in our own lives.

---

[2] Wikipedia.com
[3] Thefreedictionary.com (with my own summary)

14

Chapter 2: We Found Water

Isaac and those with him had made a decision to not settle in the valley but rather to continue their journey of discovering God's presence and blessing for themselves. I find it quite interesting that the first well of water that they rediscovered was found in the valley. Genesis 26 tells us that *"Isaac's servants dug in the valley and discovered a well of fresh water there."* So many times we assume that we have to leave the valley before we can discover God or find anything of use or value. As we considered in Chapter One, however, the lessons we can learn and the things we can discover in the valley can prove to be invaluable.

The principle for us here is that no matter where we find ourselves we can search out or dig for God. He is able to be found no matter where we find ourselves. The Psalmist declared it like this:

Where can I go from Your Spirit? Or where can I flee from Your presence? If I ascend to heaven, You are there; if I make my bed in Sheol, behold, You are there. If I take the wings of the dawn, if I dwell in the remotest part of the sea, even there Your hand will lead me, and Your right hand will lay hold of me.
Psalm 139:7-10

We Should Find it Here

By its very nature and meaning, a valley would be a narrow place where a brook would run. We discussed how in Gerar it was not so; rather it was a dry place. Although on the surface the Valley of Gerar presented itself as a dry place, Isaac and his men understood that in this place they should be able to find a brook or a source of water.

The Philistines had covered over the wells of Abraham. The enemy had worked hard to keep the wells from producing and providing in the ways in which they were designed to produce. Even the valley itself had been affected in that it was not living up to its name or potential. So often we find ourselves in a situation that in reality should be a particular way, but the way it appears is contrary to the way it should be. The reason oftentimes is that so many things have been misused, abused or covered over by the enemy that potential and productivity have been lost altogether.

The most fascinating part is that Isaac and his men knew they should be able to find water in this valley. They were able to see beyond the circumstance and realize the true potential of the situation. How many times have we looked at a situation as hopeless because everyone else has seen it and proclaimed it hopeless? How many times do we fail to realize what is available, what has been hidden or covered over? Many times we find ourselves in a valley, a place that the enemy wants to convince us as having no potential for productivity. Instead of realizing the truth from God's perspective, we follow in the ways of many before us and miss the productivity of the valley.

There are times we find ourselves in situations where it does not make sense to keep digging or to keep going. Why dig when we are already in a valley – when it already feels that we are as low as we can go? There was a moment in my life at the ripe old age of twenty that I had to decide how I was going to respond in my valley.

Have you ever prayed for and believed God for something and then had it turn out differently than you hoped or wanted? I am pretty sure all of you would say yes and therefore you know what I mean.

There are times in life when you feel as though you know without question what is best and the only person that seems to not agree with you is God. Those moments are frustrating, as He ultimately has the final say. You see, I can tell God what I want. I can tell God what I think. But I cannot tell God what to do. With my personality that can be a very tough pill to swallow.

I will never forget the empty feeling in the pit of my stomach when my nephew passed away on Christmas Day 1997. It was the most gut wrenching moment of my life. I had just recently given my life to God and made a commitment to serve Him and preach His Word. I was in the middle of a wonderful time in my life: I was training for ministry service at Brownsville Revival School of Ministry, in the midst of the greatest church revival in our day.

When I learned of the diagnosis, I had mixed feelings. I was shocked. But at the same time, I was confident that God was going to take care of the situation. Because I knew that the Bible said "With people this is **impossible**, but with God all things are **possible**." (Matthew 19:26) I had no reason to think or believe otherwise.

So I prayed and believed. I fasted and believed. I worshiped and believed. I laid hands on and believed. Then I stood and wept at his casket. In my young Christian mind something did not seem to make sense. What had just happened? Where did God go? Why did He let me down?

I remember feeling so dejected and disappointed. I remember thinking that I was a fool for ever believing God could do something that, with man, truly was impossible. I found myself questioning everything I had just started to truly

17

believe. I was at a crossroads in my life and I did not know what to do about it.

So I began to read the Bible more fervently. I told God I desperately needed Him to help me make sense of things. I missed Matt. For 19 years we had done nearly everything together. I was not sure how to operate without knowing he was there. I asked God if He had any idea what I was feeling. Know what? He did know. And He showed me that He understood. My life changed when I read this:

Now when Jesus heard about John, He withdrew from there in a boat to a secluded place by Himself; and when the people heard of this, they followed Him on foot from the cities. When He went ashore, He saw a large crowd, and felt compassion for them and healed their sick.
Matthew 14:13-14

Jesus had just heard about the beheading of his cousin John the Baptist. They had grown up together and spent lots of time together. They had a bond as relatives that cannot be manufactured. And, when Jesus heard that John had died He withdrew to be alone. He withdrew because He was sad. He withdrew because for the first time in His life He was going to be without his cousin.

But Jesus did not get trapped in His time of mourning and sadness. He ministered to others who were in need. He continued to do what He had been created to do. I learned a valuable lesson in those two verses – life is not about what happens to us, but how we respond to what happens to us.

I decided to dig in my valley. From that day on, I have dedicated myself to doing everything I can to help people. I want to have a positive impact on everyone with whom I come into contact. I want to be moved with compassion for others and to help them find the healing they need.

As much as I miss my nephew - my best friend - I am thankful for the important lesson I learned after he was gone. I learned the value of pressing on and doing what I am made to do. And you can do the same. I may not be able to personally relate to your story. I will not lie to you and tell you I completely understand or have found myself in your specific valley. I can relate in a general sense, however, as I have been there. I do know the desire to freeze up or give up in the moment of despair and disappointment.

I also know that I am a better person for what I have experienced. And I know that God has comforted me time and again in the midst of difficulty and disappointment. Time and again I am reminded of this important calling that I MUST fulfill:

Blessed be the God and Father of our Lord Jesus Christ, the Father of mercies and God of all comfort, who comforts us in all our affliction so that we will be able to comfort those who are in any affliction with the comfort with which we ourselves are comforted by God.
2 Corinthians 1:3-4

God is sovereign. God is supreme. God is the ultimate authority. We will never fully understand His ways. God will never be predictable but He will always be trustworthy. He will always be there for *you* even if it feels He was not there for the *situation*.

How Do We Dig?

What does this mean? It is one thing to realize our position and our need to dig, but what do we do next? I am fine with having someone encourage and motivate me to action. Yet so often we fail to empower people for action and just employ them to action. Through this book, my hope is to help us to realize the tools available to make our digging successful.

So what does it mean to dig? How do we dig to find what it is God has promised or what it is that we feel God wants us to find? How do we take up this proverbial shovel and begin our quest? We D.I.G. Let us consider this acronym to better understand what it means to just keep digging.

Dig with Desire

By nature you will never go after something you do not want. If a person is content in their valley, he will never begin digging to find anything different. You must want it. To desire something is to want or long for it. It is an insatiable appetite that motivates a person to action to find or possess the object of his affection or desire.

In a lot of ways society has twisted the concept of desire. Many see or hear that word and their minds and attitudes can quickly become uncomfortable or defensive. I am not speaking of being lustful. I am not speaking of unnatural affections. I am speaking of a healthy ambition or God-given appetite to go after something that you do not currently have in your possession, but that which you know God wants you to have.

I am not referring to coveting or wanting something beyond God's provision. What I am saying is that we must be a people who dig with desire and passion to find God – His presence, His blessing, His provision. If you hand someone a shovel in the natural and they have no desire for what needs to be found, it will be reflected in their work. However, if you have found the "X" on the treasure map, watch the dirt begin to fly as the digging is done with eagerness and urgency.

Isaac had made a heart level commitment to uncover the wells of his father. That is the seat of desire – it must be heart level. So many times we determine to do something from a conscious or mind level and seldom truly complete it. Why? The desire just is not there and it quickly fades. This is a God-established principle. Through the prophet Jeremiah, God declared:

You will seek Me and find Me when you search for Me with all your heart.
Jeremiah 29:13

This screams of desire. Half-hearted effort produces half-finished results. Think about Noah and the ark. Imagine if he had only invested halfway in the building of the ark. He was fully committed to complete that for which God had commissioned him, and the results speak for themselves. Sometimes I wonder how many half-finished arks or half-dug wells people have in their lives.

Isaac and his men found water, because they had a desire to find water. They were not going to settle for just finding dirt, they desired to find water. And that leads to the second factor to consider in our digging.

Dig with Intent

If you are going to dig, it helps to know that for which you are digging. Intentional digging is much more effective than random or haphazard digging. It does not take much effort to find dirt when you dig. Isaac and his men were digging with the intent to find water. To do something with intent means that you are committed or resolute in your action and unwilling to settle for less.

A recent memory of digging was when I dug the hole for our mailbox post. I knew how deep the hole needed to be and I knew what I needed to do to get to that point. However, it seemed as though my manual post-hole diggers kept running out of gas. Have you ever been there? But I knew that if I did not dig deep enough there was a very real possibility that my mailbox was going to be unsecure and unstable. It was necessary for me to be committed and steadfast in reaching the desired and needed depth.

We were living in southern Kentucky at the time, and I must say that digging in red clay and rock is neither pleasant nor easy. There are times when the digging is difficult and the desire can wane or shift toward stopping the process. Yet, when your focus is fixed on the prize, you just keep digging. The Apostle Paul said it like this:

Brethren, I do not regard myself as having laid hold of it yet; but one thing I do: forgetting what lies behind and reaching forward to what lies ahead, I press on toward the goal for the prize of the upward call of God in Christ Jesus.
Philippians 3:13-14

Do you know why Isaac found water when he and his men dug in the valley? They were looking for water. When you are intent on what it is that you are after, you will find it. Misguided and misplaced intent will find nothing because it is in pursuit of nothing. If you lack intent you will lack results. If the resolve and the focus are missing, then you are sure to find the nothing for which you are looking. But when you focus, when you set your gaze and make your path sure, you will uncover that for which you are in pursuit. And you will do so even if it is difficult, which establishes the last element of digging.

Dig with Guts

If desire and intent are missing you are going to give up when things become difficult. However, when desire and intent are present, they will be accompanied by the guts needed to complete the task and pursuit. Understand that I am not speaking about being foolish. There can be a fine line between faith and foolishness. But there are times when acting or continuing to act in faith may not make much sense. Yet those who approach the pursuit with spirit and spunk are those who find the well of water.

Consider the account of Gideon and his army. They had been given an important assignment by God. Their desire and intent was to be victorious. However, the reality was that they were outnumbered and destined for defeat. Nonetheless these men operated in guts. The account of this story in Judges 6-8 is a fascinating look at the power of the fortitude of man. I particularly love this statement about Gideon and his men.

Then Gideon and the 300 men who were with him came to the Jordan and crossed over, weary yet pursuing.
Judges 8:4

The heart and the courage of an individual or a group are not to be defeated by weariness. The gutsy do not allow circumstances or difficulty to steal their passionate pursuit. The Apostle Paul told the Galatians to *"not lose heart in doing good, for in due time we will reap if we do not grow weary"* (Galatians 6:9).

23

Isaac's servants dug in the valley and discovered a well of
fresh water there.
Genesis 26:19

Isaac's servants discovered a well of fresh water. Why were they able to discover this well? Because they dug. They dug with a desire to find water. They dug with the intent to find water. And they dug with the guts to keep digging until they found water. They understood that in the valley they were supposed to find a brook, a source of water. They understood that on the surface Gerar was dry. If they were willing to dig below the surface they would uncover something fresh and nourishing. That is exactly what they did. In the midst of your valley – DIG. In the midst of your dry time – DIG. Wherever you find yourself – DIG.

In the coming chapters we will continue to see the importance of desire, intent and guts. We do not just need these qualities as we begin to dig; we need these qualities to just keep digging.

Section 2: Waters of Esek

Isaac reopened the wells that had been dug in the time of his father Abraham, which the Philistines had stopped up after Abraham died, and he gave them the same names his father had given them. Isaac's servants dug in the valley and discovered a well of fresh water there. But the herders of Gerar quarreled with those of Isaac and said, "The water is ours!" So he named the well Esek, because they disputed with him.
Genesis 26:18-20

Esek is defined as contention and comes from the root word for strife. This is the only use of this word in the Old Testament.

The geographical location of Esek is unknown.

Chapter 3: We Were Not Looking for the Quarrel

Isaac's servants dug in the valley and discovered a well of
fresh water there. But the herders of Gerar quarreled with
those of Isaac and said, "The water is ours!" So he named the
well Esek, because they disputed with him.
Genesis 26:19-20

So let me get this straight. Isaac and his servants
decided they were not going to settle in the valley of dryness
but rather they were going to dig to find something better from
God only to find quarreling and contention? How is that even
possible? Is it safe to say that many of us often assume that
simply because we move forward things are automatically
going to work and become easier? In a perfect world, Isaac
and his men would have dug in the valley and found the ideal
well of water. But the story does not end with just one dig.

First, Isaac and his servants were greeted by the well of
fresh water – the object of their desire and the reason they
began to dig in the first place. Then, they were confronted
with the herders of Gerar who began to quarrel over the well
and declare that they somehow owned it. Is it not frustrating
that the people who did the work to find the water were
instantly attacked by those who somehow felt they owned or
deserved the water, but had done nothing to discover it? Is
this not a deep challenge we often face in our lives? We
press in and discover something that we worked for and then
someone else decides to stake a claim to it. This will
challenge us to the core. How are we going to respond?

The root of what we find at Esek is an argumentative
encounter. The people who quarreled with Isaac and his men
did not seem to care much about the men or the region until
the water was discovered. That is what brought about the

argument and strife. While the geographical location of Esek is not clear, it is clear that it was a place of contention. Upon discovering the water and the blessing of God, Isaac, representing the people of God, quickly met an adversary.

Our Adversary is Prowling

As you individually or even as an entire church begin to discover God's wells of blessing, you too can count on contention from an adversary. Peter says it in this manner:

Be of sober spirit, be on the alert. Your adversary, the devil, prowls around like a roaring lion, seeking someone to devour.
1 Peter 5:8

Peter depicts the devil as our adversary, and as one who is prowling about like a lion looking for prey to devour. Typically when you find a lion hunting prey, the lion will get as close as possible to the prey under some type of cover or darkness. The lion will look for isolated prey or at times prey that are in the process of enjoying some type of spoil of their own. Once near enough to their prey, the lion will quickly rush and pounce on the prey in an attempt to startle and kill. Does not that sound much like what our own adversary the devil does? Is it any wonder, then, that Peter describes the devil in that manner?

Isaac and his men had just discovered a fresh well. They had just reconnected with God's blessing that had been upon his father, Abraham. They were ready to enjoy the spoils of their labor. Yet, they encountered dissension and strife. The men in the region had become so accustomed to controlling the land and region that even when the rightful owners returned and rediscovered the blessing, they were quick to contend.

I see such a fascinating parallel here. There are things that the enemy has unrightfully taken as his own possession. There are people, places and even regions that belong to God's people in both a spiritual and a historical sense. Yet the enemy believes them to be his possession. And when the people of God begin to turn back and rediscover that which was lost or forgotten, they are sure to be confronted with strife and contention from the enemy. He simply is not going to roll over, play dead and welcome you back.

The root of this word "Esek" is "strife," and this is the only time that we find this word being used in the Old Testament. It speaks of contention, strife, judgment, quarreling, complaining and dispute. It clearly denotes difficulty and opposition. While we might like to think our adversary is going to sit back and watch as we begin to move forward in the things of God that simply is not true. It may be more appealing to think, believe or even say that as our relationship with God grows we will only experience His blessing – that is simply not the case. The Kingdom of God is marked by opposition. Please understand that our adversary the devil is not the opposite of God, for God has no opposites. However, he is clearly in opposition to God and to God's people. As such he will continuously do his part to try and stop what God and His people are trying to do.

The number one agenda of the men who rose in opposition at the waters of Esek was to get Isaac and his men to quit digging and to simply hand the rediscovered blessing over to them. By opposing Isaac and his men, the men of Gerar expected to maintain control of the well. The desire of the enemy was to convince Isaac that his effort in digging the well was a waste of time. He wanted the opposition that arose as a result of the digging to appear to Isaac as greater than the blessing they had discovered by digging.

The screaming attempt against Isaac and his family and friends was, "To be dry and thirsty is better than the problems brought on by the water you find when you dig." That is so often the ploy of Satan in our lives as well. The adversary would love nothing more than to convince us that it would be better to never dig at all than to dig and encounter opposition. If he can convince you and me that the process of digging in and going deeper in God is not worth it, then he can defeat us and bring us to a place of dryness and ineffectiveness. He desires to cause us to see the costs of the blessing as greater than the benefit of the blessing. His ultimate desire is for us to believe that following Christ is too difficult and not worth the effort. With that in mind he looks to bring great strife and contention into our lives.

Can You See it Coming?

I wonder if Isaac and the others were surprised by the opposition they faced. Or did they anticipate it? I once heard a story about a young man who decided to join the military. His motivation was to have something to fill his time, a stable form of income, and a free education. Those factors are what primarily drove him to enlist. Following his basic training there came a point where he and his group were sent to a base in Korea. He was frantically looking for someone who could help him understand what was going on, and why he was going to another country to take part in a combat mission. In his words, "I did not sign up for this!"

How many of the men with Isaac thought that very thing as the men of Esek began to quarrel with them over the waters? Did they question whether or not it was worth it? Did

29

they think to themselves or out loud, "I only signed up to dig and drink?" Again I ask were they surprised by the opposition.

What about you or me? Do we step into a new place of blessing with God and encounter opposition from the adversary and declare, "I did not sign up for this?" Do we find ourselves questioning the value of what we are experiencing in light of what we are facing? As a pastor I have come to understand something. It is much more popular, favorable and even easier to declare that in Christ we only experience His blessing and His best. It is much more appealing to all of us to think, believe and declare that there will never be any opposition if we live right.

In fact, is this not what I call the friends of Job factor? Do you remember how they were constantly reminding Job that if only he were righteous before God all would be well? This is not a new or foreign concept. It is quite popular and it makes for a great conference, or a book or sermon series, which can be mass produced and loved by the crowd. However, where is the reality of that?

I am not implying that there are not blessings to be found in the presence of the Lord and in being in right relationship with Him. But I am not going to pretend that there is only good and that there is never any opposition or adversity. Sometimes when you press in and dig in to find what God has for you there is going to be some difficult opposition that arises as a result. How many in the church world today would ridicule the Apostle Paul for facing some of the trials and difficulties he faced because of his faith? Yet consider what Paul declared to Timothy in his letter,

Indeed, all who desire to live godly in Christ Jesus will be persecuted.
2 Timothy 3:12

I am not trying to promote suffering for the sake of suffering. I do not enjoy it when I face opposition and challenges. But we must realize that Esek represents an important principle for us to understand and embrace. As we uncover the blessing of God, the last thing the adversary is going to do is sit idly by, allowing us to simply enjoy what he believes belongs to him. Peter declares this:

Dear friends, do not be surprised at the fiery ordeal that has come on you to test you, as though something strange were happening to you.
1 Peter 4:12 (NIV)

Be encouraged in knowing that when the enemy opposes you it means you must be a threat to him. On Christmas Day, 1997, I lost the best friend I had ever known on this earth. My nephew, Matt, left this world as a result of an ongoing battle with brain cancer. Rarely a day goes by that I do not remember him and some of the things we did together (some of which I better not recount). He was nineteen years old when he passed away. During the latter portion of his life Matt kept a journal where he would draw, write poems or share his thoughts and feelings. I want to close out this chapter with a statement from his journal that will stick with me for the rest of my life. In light of what Isaac and his men faced and in light of what we have talked about throughout this chapter, it feels like an appropriate way to conclude. Matt said this,

"If you have never met the devil face to face, it probably means you are going the same way he is."

Chapter 4: Just Keep Digging

But the herders of Gerar quarreled with those of Isaac and
said, "The water is ours!" So he named the well
Esek, because they disputed with him. Then they dug another
well . . .
Genesis 26:20-21

The statement that jumps out to me the most is the first part of verse 21, "Then they dug another well." Isaac and his friends did not back down or give up when opposition arose. They dug in even further. Very few places will teach us more about ourselves than the classroom of adversity. How we respond can have a lasting effect on where we go from that point. What far too many of us do is exactly what the enemy wants – we throw up our hands and quit, deciding that the challenges are too difficult to face.

In Chapter Two we explored the nature of digging by using the acronym D.I.G. This is a good place for a recap. We must dig with **Desire**. We must be passionate about and in pursuit of what we are expecting to receive from God. Isaac and those with him willed themselves to keep pursuing God's blessing.

Consider Laura for a moment. Laura is a fascinating lady in our church. She has been through so much in her life, and has experienced God's freedom and deliverance on levels that many would have a hard time understanding. Both she and her husband, Davis, are extremely passionate in their pursuit of God. They are diggers. And they dig with desire. She made a comment to me once that sums up digging with desire. Laura said this, *"many are will not's as the percentage of can not's is miniscule."* The question is rarely whether or not a person "can," but whether or not a person "will."

Secondly, we must dig with **Intent**. It is important that we be determined and committed to discover what God has for our lives. The men who quarreled over the waters of Esek were intent in their opposition. They determined that their rights to the waters were greater than Isaac's. We never have to wonder if our adversary is intent or steadfast in his efforts to keep us from experiencing what God has in store for our lives. He wants nothing more than to stop us from receiving or experiencing God's best. But our focus must be fixed and secure. Once we have counted the cost and determined the worth of the blessing, we must press in and dig with intent until we uncover God's blessing.

Finally, we must dig with **Guts**. We must have the heart and courage to neither give up, nor back down regardless of what we face. As the old saying goes, "When the going gets tough, the tough get going." At times the pursuit of what God has can be fearful or even intimidating. That is why the journey is not for the faint of heart.

Following the death of Moses, it became the duty of Joshua to lead the Israelites into their Promised Land. Over and over in Joshua 1 we find God telling Joshua to "be strong and courageous." God was telling Joshua it was going to take some guts, some intestinal fortitude, to lead His people and to accomplish what God had prepared. And when we have the benefit of looking at the entire story from start to finish, God was being brutally honest with Joshua. There were moments along the way where it would have been very easy and very tempting to walk away. Yet Joshua held onto God's call to courage, and he fulfilled his purpose in leading God's people. But the entire time it took a lot of guts.

Can you picture Joshua at the moment when he knew it was his responsibility to lead the people? Can you say knot in the stomach or throat? I figure the reason God had to continually remind him to be strong and courageous is that Joshua wanted to run and hide. He had been around and seen Moses get frustrated and struggle with these people. How were things with him going to be any different or better? Joshua must have been in a constant mental struggle as to whether or not he was capable of accomplishing the task to which God had called him. Did he truly have the guts needed?

How often do we deal with the same internal struggles? If we are not careful, we can become so wrapped up in recalling or recounting the struggles of others, that we assume our path is not going to be any better. But God has called each of us to dig and pursue His purpose for our lives. We cannot afford to entangle ourselves with either comparison or assumption. We simply must move forward with deep and consistent resolve to see God's plan fulfilled.

Are Things Ever Different?

Something significant took place when Isaac began to dig the wells. If we are not careful, it is both something we can miss from this story as well as something we can do ourselves. Look closely:

Isaac reopened the wells that had been dug in the time of his father Abraham, which the Philistines had stopped up after Abraham died, and he gave them the same names his father had given them.
Genesis 26:18

Did you catch the significant statement at the end of that verse? Isaac *"gave them the same names his father had given them."* Is it not interesting how often we expect history to repeat itself? Notice I did not say how often history does repeat itself, but how often we expect it to repeat itself.

We do not have any clear Scriptural backing concerning the names given the wells by Abraham, other than reading here that Isaac gave them the same names as his father. Therefore, we must assume that Esek was the name Abraham had given the well. And the definition of Esek did not suddenly change with Isaac. I cannot help but wonder if Isaac and his men anticipated the quarreling that took place at the well of Esek. Did they predetermine that they were going to face strife and contention? Were they obligated to face the strife and contention or was it simply a matter of their expectations being met? Think for a moment about how often you and I do the same thing.

We find ourselves about to do something for God, and the first thing we begin to do is think about what happened to others in the past when they did that very thing. Surely if the men quarreled with Abraham they are going to quarrel with Isaac. Surely if the Israelites continually gave Moses ulcers why would things be any different with Joshua? In essence we can often put ourselves into a defeated position before we even give the battle a chance to unfold.

Do we sometimes fail to realize that God just might want to do something different this time? Are we convinced that everything is going to be a cookie cutter experience? And since we cannot see any change or difference we may as well embrace the inevitable? Is it possible for us to box ourselves into the results by deciding we have seen it all before? What if instead of naming the well Esek, or quarrel, he had named the well after himself – Isaac, which means laughter? Paul makes a powerful declaration about God in Romans 4.

God, who gives life to the dead and calls into being that which does not exist.
Romans 4:17

God is unlimited in His potential and power. He is not confined to any parameters or plan. Yes, I realize that He is the same yesterday, today and forever (Hebrews 13:8). I understand that God does not change like shifting shadows (James 1:17). Yet if you spend enough time in relationship with God, you begin to quickly realize and understand that He is also consistently unpredictable. He is faithful and trustworthy, but He is completely unable to be put inside a box. The moment we can describe God is the moment He ceases to be God. Yet so often we put limitations on Him by assuming we know the end of the story. Isaac named the wells the same thing as Abraham. Where was the creativity to see things differently?

Early in ministry I encountered a very interesting situation. I had encouraged the people to be actively looking for someone in their lives who could mentor them, as well as someone to whom they could be a mentor. A gentleman told me he had a real problem with that idea. I asked him why. He was completely convinced that there was not a single person in the church that was capable of mentoring him. In other words, he had it all figured out and he had it all together. That is a very sad place to find one's self. When we are not teachable, we are not reachable. When we are not teachable, we are no longer able to teach.

The purpose of this book is persistence and perseverance toward discovering what God has for us. God is the God who is able to change course and He holds all things under His authority and control. That includes you. Do not underestimate Who God is in you or who you are in God. So much of life is about perspective. So many times we live with tunnel vision and the inability to see beyond what we have always experienced. We live with things as we declare them to be. Rather than endure from our limited perspective, what if we call things by a different name? Instead of speaking death what if we learn to speak that which brings life? Perhaps then we enjoy what God brings into our lives rather than always having to endure what we bring upon ourselves.

The Art of Perseverance

Regardless of how or why the men ended up at Esek, they kept digging. Genesis recounts, *"then they dug another well."* Whether or not they expected the resistance at Esek they got it. Regardless of what they thought might take place next, they kept digging.

Perseverance is defined as steady persistence in a course of action, a purpose or a state, especially in spite of difficulties, obstacles or discouragement. [4] Perseverance is not always an easy or automatic thing. We are not naturally wired to keep going when we encounter difficulties. It involves a choice of our will. It requires us to get up, dust ourselves off and go for it again and again. Two verses that consistently come to mind in light of perseverance are found in Proverbs 24.

If you are slack in the day of distress, your strength is limited....For a righteous man falls seven times, and rises again, but the wicked stumble in time of calamity.
Proverb 24:10, 16

I do not want to live my life with limited strength. I do not want to stumble in the day of calamity or difficulty. I want

---

[4] Dictionary.com

to be the righteous man that rises again and continues to persevere regardless of how difficult I may perceive things to be. To operate in steady persistence is often the difference between success and failure. It is often said about athletes that those who persist and continue to stay the course are the ones who prove to be the most successful. Imagine if Michael Jordan had quit playing basketball because he did not make his high school team? How much different would the landscape of the game of basketball, and specifically basketball in Chicago, look as a result?

There are times that we encounter challenges and setbacks and giving up or giving in can be the natural tendency. But what we must do is press in, press on, and press through until we find that for which we are searching.

But What If . . .

For the next few moments let us consider what is often the greatest battle and obstacle to continuing to dig. I am speaking of doubt. So many times when we begin our journey toward what we believe God has available to us, we will encounter a time of doubting, second guessing and playing the "what if" game. I often find, however, that doubt is very misunderstood.

We often assume that doubt is the opposite of faith, when in reality doubt is an obstacle to faith that must be overcome. The opposite of faith is unbelief, and if left unchecked doubt can serve to build a bridge from faith to unbelief. Yet doubt is not particularly wrong. Doubt can actually prove to be a valuable teacher and aid in perseverance. Many of the spiritual battles we win in our lives are a result of our ability to work through and overcome the

38

questions and doubt that arise. In this way doubt can actually be used to our advantage.

I like this quote from Winkie Pratney's book, _The Thomas Factor,_ "Although everyone has experienced it, few people today have thought deeply about doubt. It is one of the most misunderstood problems in life. We always tend automatically to equate doubt with unbelief. It is not the same thing at all!"[5]

James 1:8 tells us that a double-minded man is unstable in all his ways. Double-mindedness speaks of uncertainty or wavering about which way to go or what to do. But also keep this principle in mind: uncertainty after the decision is second-guessing; uncertainty before the decision is doubt. We can often spend so much of our time in doubt and inactivity that we never need to second-guess anything. I have often told our church that I would rather fail while trying than to succeed while doing nothing. We must be careful that we do not allow doubt to immobilize us.

The key is to understand that doubt is a common feeling or situation in which we find ourselves. The issue is never about whether or not we are going to feel or experience doubt. The issue is always whether or not we remain in that place of doubt and allow ourselves to become immobilized.

What might have happened to Isaac if, after Esek, he and his men had doubted whether or not it was worth moving forward? What if they had determined that even digging Esek was a mistake and so there was no need to even consider digging any further? What if you and I do that in our own lives? How many of us **have** done that in our own lives?

---

[5] Winkie Pratney, "The Thomas Factor: The Key to Believing When You Cannot Find an Answer"

The Josiah Factor

In 1999, my wife and I said "I DO" and committed our lives to one another. We were both in our early twenties at the time and had all of these wonderful plans for our future. Of course, our short term future included children. We decided that we would spend two years together as husband and wife and then bring our first child into our family. It seemed like the most logical plan. Even before we were married I always viewed Kim as a mother without any children. She just has that quality about her, that you know motherhood is a strong purpose for her. In 2001, we decided it was time to put our plan into action. Our first son, Josiah, was born in 2008. For those that are not the best at math, this did not add up with our plan. We thought that by the time 2008 rolled around we would have two children, with a possible third on the way.

I must say that in terms of family dynamic, those were the longest, most grueling and most gut wrenching years of my life. I cannot tell you how many negative pregnancy tests we took. I cannot tell you how many times we cried on one another's shoulders over the disappointment. As months of what we deemed failure turned to years, we had crossed the bridge from belief about having children to firmly believing it was never going to happen. The bridge from faith to unbelief that was paved by doubt was fully traveled in our hearts and minds.

Doubt will test and prove the strength of your faith in God. What is it to which you are truly committed? In or on what are you truly relying?

Our plan was not working. And it caused us to wonder about everything we believed. Doubt had given way to bitterness and disappointment with God. We could not figure out why God was not giving us a child. It did not make sense to us. The bottom line was that we had a decision to make. We were being pressed by life and what was on the inside, in our hearts, was being shown to us.

I remember doing something that did not make sense to me at the time, but it was something I knew and believed I had to do. I went to a local store and purchased a boy's and a girl's baby bib to give to Kim as a Christmas present. I remember putting them in a gift bag and when she opened them she gave me a look I will never forget. I took her by the hand and I said, "I still believe, and no matter what it takes, we are going to have a baby." There was something supernatural in that moment. Together we determined to just keep digging. The following September, nine months later, we welcomed our son, Josiah, into the world.

"Commitment cements belief into conviction."[6]

The joy of the positive pregnancy test can never be accurately stated. Being a man of great faith and trust, I was just as excited for the second and third home pregnancy test, as well as the doctor confirmed blood test. We had kept digging and we found life!

I once preached a series on faith as relayed in Hebrews 11. In studying the story of Abraham and Sarah believing God for the promised birth of Isaac, I realized something very important. It is one thing to accept God's Word. It is something entirely different to align yourself with His Word by your actions. Romans 4 says that Abraham's body was as good as dead. Genesis tells us that Sarah was barren and

---

[6] Winkie Pratney "The Thomas Factor: The Key to Believing When You Cannot Find an Answer".

beyond the time of bearing children. Yet God spoke to them and promised them that they would give birth to a son.

It was necessary for Abraham and Sarah to align themselves with God's promise through their action. We cannot miss the fact that in order for Isaac to be conceived, Abraham and Sarah had to have sex. In that moment we find the valuable principle of aligning ourselves with what God has spoken. The facts said that Abraham and Sarah were going to be childless forever. But THE TRUTH had spoken that they would conceive a son named Isaac.

Without their act of faith there would be no Isaac. Without Isaac there would have been no digging of the wells. Without the digging of the wells you would be doing something other than reading this book at this moment. Yet Abraham and Sarah took hold of futures realities in their present moment by aligning themselves with what God had spoken.

Get Your Shovel

Isaac and the men with him had been so excited when they found the water. Yet they encountered quarrelling and opposition. They must have felt disappointment and doubt creeping in, causing them to wonder if there was any reason to keep digging. But that is exactly what they did.

It does not matter what you find along the way – keep digging.
It does not matter what obstacles stand in your way –
keep digging.
And when you think there is no more that you can take –
keep digging.
Just keep digging.

Section 3: Waters of Sitnah

Then they dug another well, but they quarreled over that one also; so he named it Sitnah.
Genesis 26:21

Sitnah is defined as hostility.

Sitnah is derived from the same root as Satan.

Sitnah speaks of adverse conditions or opposition that one faces from the adversary himself.

Chapter 5: Are You Kidding Me?

*Then they dug another well, but they quarreled over that one
also; so he named it Sitnah.*
Genesis 26:21

On the heels of Isaac's determining to move forward
and dig again, they encountered Sitnah. The name Sitnah is
derived from the same root word from which we get the name
Satan. It literally speaks of dealing with an adversary. You
might even say that the things left undone by Esek were
attacked and battled at Sitnah.

Does that not seem like reality at times? We determine
to move forward and show perseverance, only to find even
more opposition. It often seems that the more we fight and
work, the more we are forced to fight and work. There are
times when we would do just about anything for some type of
break. Keep that thought in mind when we move into Section
Four and consider Rehoboth.

Sitnah represents the place that we so often quit in our
pursuit. We fought so hard to overcome the strife and
contention of Esek, only to find ourselves face to face with the
adversary himself at Sitnah. It is as if all Hell has broken
loose in our lives. How many of us have ever said, "Whatever
can go wrong will go wrong?" The onslaught that seems to be
never-ending can be debilitating, rendering us hopeless or
helpless.

Consider two prime Scriptures that address the nature
of our own spiritual adversary – Satan.

Jesus said:

The thief comes only to steal and kill and destroy; I came that they may have life, and have it abundantly.
John 10:10

And, Peter said:

Be of sober spirit, be on the alert. Your adversary, the devil, prowls around like a roaring lion, seeking someone to devour.
1 Peter 5:8

We gain some valuable insight concerning our adversary. Jesus said he came to steal, kill and destroy. Peter said he is seeking someone to devour. It is obvious that our adversary is not operating with our best interest in mind. Take a moment and consider these words used to describe Satan's plan of action against you and me.

Steal

The word used here is *klepto*, from which we get our word kleptomaniac. The image is of someone stealing secretively or by stealth. I imagine that following Esek, Isaac and his men must have expected to find some relief. However, what they found was Sitnah. Satan is labeled a "thief." Peter declares that Satan is prowling about looking for someone to devour. The plan of the adversary is to completely steal away everything good from your life.

When you consider what it means to steal something, it denotes taking away from someone something that they already have. It is a removal of something from a person's past that is in their possession and in some ways defines who they are. When something is stolen away, the item is not the

45

only thing that is taken. There is also a sense of the loss of security through theft.

In essence what our adversary wants to do is this: Satan wants to remove from you that which you earned, that which is in your possession, and that which defines some or all of who you are. In the process he wants to take away your sense of security and safety, leaving you with a feeling that nothing is protected or really yours to possess. Satan wants you and me to believe that at any point he can swoop in as a thief and steal away anything that he chooses.

This is the first element we see at Sitnah. At Esek, the men had declared, "The water is ours!" At Sitnah, they quarreled also. Once again they were stealing away what Isaac and his men had taken possession of – the water in the well. Sitnah is a perfect picture of the nature of our adversary to steal.

Kill

The word used here is *thuo* and it means to kill or offer as a sacrifice. The root speaks of offering something as a spiritual sacrifice, and the reference in John 10:10 speaks of killing completely. Here we see that our adversary wants to kill us completely and to treat us as a spiritual sacrifice. The enemy's intent is to sacrifice us in a way that destroys our worth and makes us an example to others.

By "worth" I mean that the adversary views you as no more important than a sacrificial pawn. While animals that were sacrificed had to be perfect and specifically chosen, there was still a devaluing of life that took place. A sacrifice was used in place of someone or something that had greater perceived value. In order for a person to not die or face the consequence of sin, an animal was sacrificed. It was

46

determined that the animal's life was of less value than the life of the person. Essentially we need to realize that the enemy views you and me as being far less valuable than his plan. He has no problem killing or sacrificing us, because to him we are worthless.

The enemy also wants to make an "example" of us by causing others to see what happens to those who oppose him. In killing or sacrificing us, the adversary is trying to make an example out of us; he is trying to convince others of his power and control. The difficulty encountered at Sitnah was a picture of the example the enemy would love to make of us. Because they persevered and moved forward, the enemy stepped hard in their path to kill or sacrifice them and get them off track.

In addition, just as something stolen is a taking away of that which a person has possessed, when you kill someone or something you take away the present state. I cannot think of anything Satan would love to do more than to stop you and me in our present state. Sitnah is like a large stop sign saying, "Thus far and no more." The one sure way to keep someone or something from moving forward is to stop them right now. If the enemy of our souls can convince us that he is an immovable object, he will successfully kill us.

Destroy

The word used here is *apollumi* and it means to fully destroy or cut off entirely. It speaks of certain demise. Jesus is saying that Satan has come with the intent of making your end and your destruction certain. As with our story in Genesis 26, one of the most common ways the enemy tries to destroy us is by persistently hounding us and causing us to second guess what we are doing.

To steal something speaks of taking something away that the person possesses, a symbol of their past being stolen. To kill is to end the present state of someone or something. And to destroy is to eliminate any potential for a future. That which has been destroyed does not have a chance to continue – it has become nonexistent. Jesus' statement about Satan indicates that he is after our past, our present and our future.

Think about what would have happened if the men with Isaac had quit digging after Esek or Sitnah. Water is essential to our existence. The enemy was literally trying to cut them off from a needed aspect of survival and life. Is this not a picture of how our adversary often deals with us? He seeks to cut us off from needed aspects of survival and life. Let me tie this together one step further. Jesus said this:

He who believes in Me, as the Scripture said, 'From his innermost being will flow rivers of living water.'
John 7:38

This river of living water speaks of a needed aspect of spiritual survival and life. Without this resource made possible by believing in and knowing Christ, our spirits will be destroyed. Our adversary is well aware of this truth, and he will go to great lengths to cut us off from any and every connection with the life given to us in Christ.

Devour

Finally, Peter said that the devil is looking for someone to devour. The word is *katapino* and it means to swallow, devour, destroy or consume. It can also speak of being overwhelmed. Our enemy is prowling about looking for someone he can overwhelm and destroy. Ultimately his tactic is to cause fear and intimidation which can serve to debilitate us, if we allow it to do so. John Bevere says it this way in his

48

book, *Breaking Intimidation*: "The root of intimidation is fear, and fear causes people to focus on themselves."[7]

If the enemy can get us focused on ourselves and afraid to keep going, his efforts to devour us will prove successful. Esek was bad and Sitnah seemed much worse. What might happen with more digging? The seeds of doubt, discouragement, and fear will cloud our mind and judgment and keep us from experiencing God's water of life, if we allow the enemy to get our eyes in the wrong place.

Victory is Available

Our adversary desires to steal away our past, to erase where we have been. His plan is to kill our present state and take away what is going on in our lives right now. He is out to destroy us, leaving us no hope for a future, and looking to devour us through fear and intimidation. Paul told Timothy that God has given us power, love and a sound mind as our weapons to combat fear (2 Timothy 1:7). This is a telltale sign in understanding the danger and power of fear in our lives. God realizes just how destructive fear can become if we allow it to remain. Therefore, He has equipped us with three powerful weapons with which to stand against fear and intimidation.

Power

We have been granted power to stand against and defeat fear. This speaks of having power or ability to be a believer. It is power based on God's ability or God's power at work in and through you and me. God's power is at work in us so that we do not have to cower to fear. The way in which we allow fear to defeat us is when we try to be victorious or

---

[7] *Breaking Intimidation* by John Bevere.

fearless in our own strength and ability. As Paul told the Philippians:

It is God who is at work in you, both to will and to work
for His good pleasure.
Philippians 2:13

Far too often we strive and try to fight this battle in our own strength and ability. Instead we need to allow the power given to us by God to be our source of strength and victory. The main reason that Isaac and the men with him were able to keep digging, even in the face of opposition, is that they were not relying on their own strength. They were on a mission to discover what God had in store for them and they were walking on that journey in God's power.

As you genuinely pursue what God has for your life, you will pursue His purpose with His power and strength and not your own.

How many times in your own life have you ceased the pursuit of something because of fear? How many times have you determined that the potential blessings and favorable results were not worth the fear and uncertainty you had to deal with in order to get there? That is what happens when you try to do things in your own strength and power. While the enemy is not going to stoop to human levels, he loves it when you or I try to battle him on human terms. So many times in my life I have found that the level of my surrender to God's strength had a direct influence on the outcome of the battle. The more frequently I surrender to and trust His power, the more frequently I experience victory.

Love

Fear can be debilitating and as John says, fear has to do with torment (see 1 John 4:18). Yet at the same time in that passage, John says that perfect love casts out fear. Here we realize our second resource in being victorious over fear – love. This is agape love or the love that centers on moral preference. This is God centered, divine love. This is the only form of perfect love that will ever cast out fear. Did you realize that perhaps the biggest difference you can ever make in someone's life is to genuinely relate the love of God to him in the midst of trial, difficulty or fear?

Let me tell you about Pastor Chris and Davis. I hold both of these men in high regard for various reasons. Both of them exemplify the love of Christ in an ongoing way. It was that personification by Chris that made an eternal impact on Davis. Prior to giving his life to Christ, Davis was a man who was given to drug abuse and violence. His checkered past kept many people at a distance, and it kept many people afraid of him in many ways. At the time, Chris was the pastor of the church that Davis was attending.

Davis has told me many times that he sensed love in the church, but felt that the love was neither extended to nor available to him. Then one day that changed. Davis asked Pastor Chris to borrow his car. Over the next five days, Davis went on a drug binge and neither Chris nor anyone else knew where he had gone. It would have been very easy to react in fear or anger to this situation. However, when Chris welcomed Davis back and showed him love, it changed Davis' life. For the first time Davis believed that the love of Christ was genuine and real. Since then, his life has never been the same.

Fear and intimidation are driven by an intense hatred. When we find ourselves afraid of someone or something, that fear can quickly develops into hatred and a desire for harm to be done to who or what has caused our fear. In fact, 2 Timothy 1:7 is the only time the word "fear" is used in the New Testament. It denotes an intensely negative feeling or emotion that drives a person to do irrational things.

Fear often causes us to become extremely critical and cutting. Most often what takes place is that we pre-determine anything and everything bad about the cause of our fear, and then focus our efforts on criticizing that person or thing. This is an important trick in the arsenal of the enemy. Ultimately what he is doing, through fear, is putting us into his own role of being an adversary. I imagine the men who quarreled with Isaac over the wells were hoping that Isaac and his men would turn on one another rather than continue their efforts of digging and pursuing what God had for them.

As my father-in-law has often said, "where love is thick faults are thin; but where love is thin, faults are thick." Oh that we would live with a thick love toward God and one another, allowing love to motivate and encourage us rather than allowing fear to destroy us.

Sound Mind

This literally means aptly acting out God's will by doing what He calls sound reasoning. I view this as the difference between reacting and responding. The law of physics tells us that for every action there is an equal and opposite reaction. Yet in many situations a reaction is not the best approach. Fear often causes us to react, and to do so based upon emotion and feelings. It is natural that when we are startled we react in a protective mode. However, with a sound mind we are to respond to fear in a way that is in line with God's will and displays sound reasoning. Whereas a reaction is a quick retaliatory action, a response is a well thought-out action that has been determined to be the best, given the circumstance or situation. Reactions may be universal and consistent, but a response will best fit the moment.

Let me contrast this for you with two well-known men from the Bible – Samson and Joseph. Samson was a strong man both in physical strength and passion. While it may be easy to say that his undoing was lustful desire for women, perhaps it would be equally appropriate to say that his undoing was being a predictable reactionary. In Judges 16, we find Delilah asking Samson over and over again to reveal to her his secret source of strength. His reaction was that he continued to play with fire. He would tell her something that was not true, and then she would use that to try and defeat him. Over and over again he allowed her to ask and dig for his secret. He was not willing to respond in the way that would have been best. Because he kept reacting the same way, he made it clear that eventually he was going to give in and reveal the truth, thus making himself weak. Our adversary will do the same with us. He will press, prod and pry to find out if we are reactionary, knowing that eventually we will cave.

On the other hand we have Joseph. After finding himself sold into slavery by his brothers, he ended up in Potiphar's house. He was very faithful and blessed of the Lord, and Potiphar gave him a great deal of authority. In Genesis 39, we find that Potiphar's wife continually tried to seduce Joseph. Yet he did not react but rather he responded. He said to her, *"How then could I do this great evil and sin against God?"* And later, as she tried again to persuade him,

53

he literally fled from the house. Joseph determined that the best response in this situation was to get as far away as he could. He fled the very appearance of evil. At that point, the only thing anyone "had" on him was lies.

The glaring difference between reacting and responding is this: when we react, we tip our hand and make ourselves weak. When we respond, we remain above reproach and force the fabrication of things against us. The weapon that God has given us in combatting the fear and intimidation of the enemy is a sound mind – the ability to respond properly.

To recap, at Sitnah the men quarreled again. Sitnah speaks of adversity, contention and strife. Sitnah is from the same root as Satan or adversary. He has come to steal, kill, destroy and devour. He delights in using fear and intimidation to not only bring us down, but to keep us there. However, God has given us the spirit of power, love and a sound mind. And Christ has promised us abundant life in Him. This means we neither have to cater to nor cower to the enemy's tactics. We can overcome and just keep digging.

Chapter 6: Just Keep Digging . . . Again

He moved on from there and dug another well.
Genesis 26:22

Here we see it again. The men had dug a second well and encountered even more trouble. At what point does enough become enough? Who has not been there? You showed resolve and strength and pressed beyond the initial challenge of strife and contention. You did not allow the setbacks at that well to keep you from moving forward and going deeper. Yet what you find is that whatever did not go wrong in Esek sure seemed to go wrong in Sitnah.

"If you have never met the devil face to face, it probably means you are going the same way he is."

As I shared earlier, my nephew made the above statement prior to his death. Our story from Genesis 26 serves as ongoing proof of the validity of that statement. I cannot tell you how many times I overcame a battle or setback only to encounter another one equally as difficult, or even more difficult, than the previous one. I heard it said that a person is either in a battle, getting ready to go into a battle, or coming out of a battle. Battles and trials are going to take place in our lives. How we respond to the battle at hand will determine the outcome of the battle.

This chapter opened with these words from Genesis 26:22 – *He moved on from there and dug another well.*

I want us to hear some very important principles of truth that are locked inside of this simple statement. If we, in our lives, can grasp these principles as we approach battles or challenges it could be the catalyst that propels us to great things in God. These words make up a part of our everyday vocabulary, yet if we slow down long enough to pay attention and grasp their importance, I truly believe something supernatural can and will take place.

He MOVED ON from there.

This is the first thing we must do – there must be a moving on if we are ever going to move forward. When an object is moving backwards, it can be said it is in decline or in retreat. When an object is standing still it becomes stagnant and dies. Therefore, forward is the only direction that produces life.

Take a moment and consider how many things in your life have been stunted or stopped by your inability to move forward. Something bad or negative took place and it left you paralyzed, in a sense, and kept you from moving on in the right direction toward the best that God had to offer you.

In *"Carrying the Torch for Revival,"* I introduced a ministry concept that I call "Faith, Forward, Freedom." This is such a vitally important concept and principle to our success as men and women of God. We can get so caught up wishing we were someone else, or thinking that we should be further along or further advanced in our faith that it causes us to stand still and do absolutely nothing to move toward life in Christ. Beginning on page 44 of that book we find this following discourse.[8]

Each of us is at a different place in our faith in God. Neither you nor I can change where we are in this moment. I cannot spend my time wishing I was further along. Where I am is where I am. I cannot change yesterday and I cannot

---

[8] Rodney Burton with Tom Stamman "Carrying the Torch for Revival"

predict tomorrow; but I can affect right now. The key is learning to find where you are now and viewing that as your starting point. Be realistic. Faith is now. Faith does not live in the past. Take a good look at yourself and realistically assess where you are in your faith. There is no condemnation or judgment needed. All that matters is where you find yourself, because that is the perfect place to be right now.

Now that we realize where we stand, it is time to move. In terms of walking with God and living our faith **there is only one direction we should be moving**. That direction is forward. We have no reason to retreat or stand still. Many of us can attest to the ineffectiveness of standing still. Therefore, our choice is forward. God is always calling us forward in our relationship with Him. This is growth. This is discipleship. This is our faith developing and allowing us to continue to do what is right in the eyes of the Lord. 2 Chronicles 34 tells us that Josiah did what was right in the eyes of the Lord and that he did so by walking it out.

The only time that you do not move forward is when you are settled into a comfort zone. I know from experience how easy it can be to let that happen. You find yourself in a place in God that is pleasant and appealing, and the easiest thing to do is to relax and become stagnant. As Jesus was transfigured before His disciples in Matthew 17 that was exactly Peter's reaction: let's pitch a tent and stay here. But when you or I stay in one place we **sacrifice God's best on the altar of His good**. We often give up so much for so little.

But what happens when we do move forward with God and we come face to face with an obstacle that seems impossible? Think for a moment about the children of Israel and their exodus from Egypt. It took a great amount of faith for them to pack up and leave what had been their home for *generations. It took a great amount of faith for them to continue to journey in obedience to God. But imagine the horror they must have felt when they found themselves stuck between the Red Sea and the Egyptian army.*

Recently the Lord asked me a question about this passage of Scripture. He asked, "Do you think I was surprised to find the Red Sea in their way?" I had never thought of it in that way. God had been leading them the entire way and had simply asked them to follow Him. He could have chosen another route that did not encounter the sea. God knew full well that His people were going to come face to face with an immovable object. As God is leading us, He is not caught off guard when we encounter challenges or obstacles. He does not fumble through a playbook to find something else to do. He does not pull together a heavenly research team to redirect the path of His people. As God saw it the Red Sea was not an obstacle, it was part of the journey. Look what Exodus says:

The angel of God, who had been going before the camp of Israel, moved and went behind them; and the pillar of cloud moved from before them and stood behind them. So it came between the camp of Egypt and the camp of Israel; and there was the cloud along with the darkness, yet it gave light at night. Thus the one did not come near the other all night.
Exodus 14:19-20

The children of Israel were led by a pillar of cloud by day and a pillar of fire by night. When the pillar moved, they would follow. The pillar would always be in front leading them. Consider this image for a moment: the Israelites are standing before the Red Sea in fear as the Egyptians are closing in from behind. The Angel of the Lord and the pillar moved behind them while they passed through the waters. That means the pillar of cloud was already crossing the Red Sea.

This was the way God was going to take His people. The Red Sea was simply part of the journey. It was not a stop sign. It was not a detour. As we move forward with God we cannot allow barriers or obstacles to stop or detour us. We should never call an obstacle what God says is an opportunity. We cannot be dictated by difficulty – but directed by Divinity.

Do you remember what Moses said to the people?

But Moses said to the people, "Do not fear! Stand by and see the salvation of the Lord which He will accomplish for you today; for the Egyptians whom you have seen today, you will never see them again forever. The Lord will fight for you while you keep silent."
Exodus 14:13-14

To Moses this seemed like the right thing to say and do. But it upset God. God was not upset that Moses told the people that God would deliver them. God was upset because Moses told the people to stand still. They were only to stand still when the pillar was not moving. The cloud was still moving, so they should be moving too. Look at God's response:

Then the Lord said to Moses, "Why are you crying out to Me? Tell the sons of Israel to go forward."
Exodus 14:15

To God, standing still was not an option. He said to go forward. The same is true for us. It does not matter if we find ourselves in a place that is comfortable or a place that is perilous; the only direction to go from that place is forward. It was only after the people stopped and Moses made his declaration that we find the pillar moved from the front to the back of the people. Their stopping was their own choice and not God's directing.

It was almost as if God was moving behind them to compel or push them forward, because they obviously were not responding to His leading in the proper manner this time. This is the only time we read about the children of Israel moving without the pillar in front of them. God's direction is always forward. And in those times when we do not follow His leading from out in front of us, He may very well move behind to compel us forward. Those steps of faith can be even more treacherous or uncertain. The best response from us is to always move forward with God leading from the front.

The result of starting from where you are in your **faith** *and moving* **forward** *is that you step into a new place of* **freedom***. For generations the children of Israel had lived in slavery in Egypt. But in that moment of walking forward they walked right into freedom.*

Thus the Lord saved Israel that day from the hand of the Egyptians, and Israel saw the Egyptians dead on the seashore.
Exodus 14:30

Regardless of the condition of the place in which you now find yourself, you do not have to stay there. You can move forward into a new place of freedom. God desires to see you move forward and progress in His Spirit to new places in Him (2 Corinthians 3:17-18). This is an ongoing and cyclical process. Once you arrive at the new place of freedom, it establishes in your life a new place of faith. That becomes your new starting point for another step forward into a new freedom, and so the cycle continues. It is a lifelong process. Each of us has to take the steps on our own and at our own pace. I encourage you to move forward. With each step Josiah took, he brought about a new freedom not only for himself but for all those under his reign. Your steps forward will impact your family, friends, neighbors, and co-workers - everyone in your life. As we move forward from faith into freedom, we find ourselves becoming more and more fruitful. God's process is perfect.

In Genesis 26 we find that Isaac and his men "MOVED ON." They were not willing to stand still and be defeated by strife and contention or by adversity. It did not make much difference to them at all what they faced; they were focused on reaching their intended destination of God's Presence. Moving on becomes much easier and much more possible when we know for certain where we are going. If you do not have a destination there is no way for you to know if you have stopped too soon.

He moved on FROM THERE.

This is so important to catch. It was not just that they moved on, but that they moved on FROM THERE. To truly move on from a place involves relocation. It was not that they kept one foot in the place they were moving on from just in case the new place did not work . . . they moved on FROM THERE.

Perhaps the greatest hindrance in a lot of people's lives is their inability to truly separate from where they have been, and move on and move forward into the new place or the next phase of their lives. We can so easily get tied into what we are used to – even if what we are used to is strife, contention or adversity. What we are facing may be a complete mess, but at least it is our complete mess. I speak from experience in this area. In far too many instances I have found myself held back by where I have been or what I have experienced, and it has prevented me from taking the necessary steps to move on from there.

The fact of the matter is that our past can either serve as an anchor or as a springboard in our lives. We can allow what we have experienced to keep us from stepping up and stepping out again. On the other hand, we can learn from the battles, challenges, failures and successes and become even better in the next place in which we find ourselves.

One of the easiest things to do is to hold on to a portion of what we have known, in case the new place to which we are moving does not seem to work out. At times in pastoral counseling you run into this approach with people. I cannot tell you how many times I have heard people say things like, "I am going to try this out and if it does not work I always have the other thing on which to fall back." While it may look like a safety net, in reality it is a crutch. Consider for a moment what Jesus said about this approach.

As they were going along the road, someone said to Him, "I will follow You wherever You go." And Jesus said to him, "The foxes have holes and the birds of the air have nests, but the Son of Man has nowhere to lay His head." And He said to another, "Follow Me." But he said, "Lord, permit me first to go and bury my father." But He said to him, "Allow the dead to bury their own dead; but as for you, go and proclaim everywhere the kingdom of God." Another also said, "I will follow You, Lord; but first permit me to say good-bye to those at home." But Jesus said to him, "No one, after putting his hand to the plow and looking back, is fit for the kingdom of God."
Luke 9:57-62

It is not that Jesus does not understand there are things we must take care of in our lives. The issue is that for some, those things have a much greater hold and pull on our lives than Christ Himself. If we are truly going to pursue Him and

62

keep digging, there are going to be things that we must move away from completely in order to fully embrace what He has for our lives. The contrast to what Jesus declared above is found in Matthew 19:

And everyone who has left houses or brothers or sisters or father or mother or children or farms for My name's sake, will receive many times as much, and will inherit eternal life.
Matthew 19:29

I can remember in my life when this verse took on a deeply personal meaning. I am the youngest child in a family with eight children. Until recently I have spent the last eleven years as the only son or daughter not living within a twenty mile radius of the other siblings. Also, my wife is the oldest child in a family with four children. She also does not live near her family. I do not say that as a mark of pride or shame. It is just the reality. We have not been separated from family because of challenges, issues or ongoing strife. The geographical separation has been entirely because of God's call to ministry that is upon our lives.

At times it has not been an easy thing to endure. In September of 2008, it became even more difficult when we welcomed our first child into the world. Yet, through all of this separation and challenge, we have known that God has been with us and has blessed us in tremendous ways. Of course we miss our families, but we do not look at them as our fallback plan.

Let me take this one step further and make it a bit more personal. In May 2011, we relocated our family to western Illinois to serve as pastors of Calvary Church. The journey to get to that point was not necessarily an easy one, however. Just five months before that we had resigned our position as pastors of a wonderful church and community. It was a gut wrenching time for us and one that had caused me to personally feel defeated. It felt as though what we had dug up and discovered had become covered over, tainted and no longer available to us.

I vividly remember having a very heartfelt, yet one-sided conversation with God. I simply told Him, "I will never pastor again." For the first time I was considering a return to family and a looking back from putting my hand to the plow. I was frustrated. I was tired. At that point I was having trouble seeing the purpose for the fight or the continued dig. Obviously, God did not honor that statement. Obviously, and thankfully, God has the final word. Over these last couple of years I have learned a valuable lesson that makes writing this book so important to me. In fact, if you only glean one thing from reading these pages I pray it is this statement.

The destination pays the price for the journey.

This is so powerful and so true. Where God is ultimately taking us is more valuable than anything we face along the journey. It seems that we often sacrifice so much for so little. How many times have you or I arrived at a destination and commented that we would not trade anything for that destination? May God help us to press in, press on and press through in every circumstance so that we do not find ourselves constantly sacrificing or giving up too soon on the best that God has for our lives.

He Dug Another Well

Do not underestimate the significance of this statement. Before we move on from this chapter, it is imperative that we realize that Isaac and his men did not only *move on from there*. They also dug another well when they arrived at the

64

next spot in the journey. The key element is the realization that moving on is only half of the process. If we move on and then do nothing, it is no better than never having moved on at all.

Isaac was one-hundred percent convinced that by digging the wells, he was going to find a connection with God like that which his father had always known. In the process of time he had realized firsthand the number of challenges along the journey. Yet none of the strife, contention or adversity was going to keep him from going further. There was a deep resolve in him to just keep digging.

Ask yourself where you are in the journey. Ask yourself what it is that the enemy is doing to convince you that the destination is not worth the effort of the journey. Ask yourself if you have the deep resolve to just keep digging.

Section 4: Waters of Rehoboth

He moved on from there and dug another well, and no one quarreled over it. He named it Rehoboth, saying, "Now the Lord has given us room and we will flourish in the land."
Genesis 26:22

Rehoboth is defined as a broad place. It is a roomy or comfortable place.

Rehoboth is a place that can be easy to settle in and find relief and a sense of accomplishment.

Rehoboth represents the place the enemy works the hardest.

Chapter 7: We Have Arrived!

He moved on from there and dug another well, and no one quarreled over it. He named it Rehoboth, saying, "Now the Lord has given us room and we will flourish in the land."
Genesis 26:22

If you are keeping score at home, the checklist goes something like this. Dig a well – check. Have the enemy confront you with strife and contention – check. Dig another well – check. Encounter deep adversity at the second well – check. Move on and dig another well – check. Isaac and his men must have anticipated the next part of the checklist to involve a plague, a war, or something completely ghastly and impossible. Yet what they found was Rehoboth – a place that represents a broad, roomy and comfortable place.

Who among us would not have responded in the same way Isaac did, by declaring, *"Now the Lord has given us room and we will flourish in the land?"* Yet in reality Isaac and his men had arrived at the most dangerous place of all. They found themselves right in the midst of a comfort zone.

Consider some interesting pieces of information about Rehoboth. Rehoboth was known as a place of deep wells that could sustain life for a very long time. It was a place that allowed for settling without too much concern. The impression was that you would always have all that you needed in Rehoboth, so why would you ever want to move on from there at all?

However, Rehoboth is also historically known as the place of the most extensive ruins. More groups and more people were ruined at Rehoboth than either of the other two places. Is it not significant that the greatest damage or loss was not incurred with strife, contention or adversity? Rather, the greatest damage or loss was incurred in the place of comfort and room. When a person settles into a comfort zone he no longer sees the need to keep digging or to go any further. From his point of view he has arrived at the best possible place.

Again we find ourselves sacrificing God's best on the altar of His good.

Think about your own life for a moment. I am confident that, like me, you can recall a moment or moments in your own life when you settled into what seemed roomy or comfortable rather than continuing to press further. It can be so easy to stop what we are doing because what we have obtained is good enough.

I believe that within the church there are two dominant attitudes or spiritual mindsets that destroy so many people. The first one is the poverty mindset. This says, "We just cannot do what we want to do because we are small." Or, "We just do not have enough money to accomplish anything for God's Kingdom." This attitude or mindset will keep a church or a group of people bound up in depression and lack for as long as they allow that mindset to remain. I could take you today to towns and cities that have fallen into this mindset and it has permeated the very core of their town. When you drive into the limits of the city you can literally feel the depression and poverty mentality that is ruling over the people.

The other attitude that follows closely on the heels of the poverty mindset is the good enough mentality. This says, "Wow! Look how far we have come. This must be our destiny." Or, "We may not be what we could be, but we are better than we were and that is good enough for us." This is the mentality most clearly represented by Rehoboth. It is roomy. It is spacious. It is seemingly void of any resistance. Having fought through the quarreling, the strife, the contention and the adversity, Rehoboth is a wonderful and welcome change. As a result we often sacrifice God's best on the altar of His good.

Pursue Peace and Not Relief

I find more and more the danger of settling for relief in lieu of peace. It can be so easy to blur the line between the two. We often find ourselves in the midst of stressful or difficult situations and all we want is some level of comfort or relief. The key is not just comfort or relief, but rather peace. More than anything else we need to find and embrace God's peace that will often "pass understanding" (Philippians 4:7). Consider the importance God places on peace.

Depart from evil and do good; seek peace and pursue it.
Psalm 34:14

The word "peace" occurs 429 times in 400 verses of the King James Bible.[9] As used here in Psalm 34, peace speaks of wholeness or health, that which is made complete. It speaks of pursuing or seeking after that which leaves nothing lacking. When you find peace that is genuine and from God you find wholeness and completion. Jesus says:

Peace I leave with you; My peace I give to you; not as the
world gives do I give to you. Do not let your heart be troubled,
nor let it be fearful.
John 14:27

---

[9] Blueletterbible.org

69

This peace given to us by Jesus will keep us from being troubled or fearful. This peace will sustain us in and through all circumstances, and is unlike anything we can find in or receive from the world. God's peace does not speak of something temporary or passing, but rather of something that sustains itself as well as the person to whom it is imparted.

Yet so often we find ourselves mistaking temporary feelings of relief for the genuine and complete peace of God. Instead of recognizing God's peace that allows us to work in and through anything we face, we are often looking for the relief or escape from the current situation. I touched on the difference in *31 Keys to Possessing Your Promise* where I outlined these key differences.[10]

Peace is the cessation of or freedom from any strife or dissension.

Relief is the alleviation, ease, or deliverance through the removal of pain, distress or oppression.

Relief can be deceiving in that you feel better just because the feeling of pain, distress, or oppression is gone. Peace is a genuine condition of the heart and spirit that can be present even if the pain, distress, or oppression remains. Relief may be the "removal of" these feelings or conditions, but peace is "freedom from" not only the conditions but also the strife that accompanies the conditions. The peace of God does not allow conditions and circumstances to have place or control over you.

What can happen is that the pain or distress leaves and we assume all is well. However, that can be one of the most dangerous places in which to find ourselves. Change and

---

[10] Rodney Burton "31 Keys to Possessing Your Promise"

growth happens in the tension and when that is relieved or eliminated it typically causes stagnation and settling. And this is the perfect description of what Rehoboth represents.

It is interesting to note that Rehoboth and its wells were historically known as being deep and plenteous, yet it is also historically known as the place of the most extensive ruins. In other words it marked the place where more people had settled down and settled in, yet never flourished or found fulfillment and completion.

Do you remember what Isaac said when they dug and found Rehoboth? *"Now the Lord has given us room and we will flourish in the land."* That sounds like a wonderful and even faith-filled declaration. However, if you listen closely you realize it was a statement made out of a feeling of relief, rather than a genuine place of peace. Isaac's declaration of flourishing was a declaration of being fruitful by way of men and animals. He was declaring that he and his men had found a place in which they could naturally flourish.

Rehoboth was a place that would allow for increase and the bearing of fruit. Rehoboth was a place that would allow for some semblance of success and growth. Rehoboth was also a place of natural blessing to dwell in at the expense of spiritual or supernatural provision and blessing. I feel like a broken record with this, but it represents a perfect opportunity to sacrifice the best for the good enough.

Easy Does Not Always Mean Right

Rehoboth offers a very difficult lesson. That which is easy is not always that which is right. It can be so deceiving to find ourselves in a relaxed or easy environment and to automatically assume or believe it is the right environment. I remember hearing Tommy Tenney say that we often find ourselves racing to false finish lines. Rehoboth is a perfect picture of that reality.

Consider the journey. Isaac and his men dug a well and discovered Esek. They were thrilled to have found water, but their thrill was soon thwarted by strife and contention when those around them claimed the water belonged to them. So they kept digging and discovered Sitnah. Once again the thrill of the discovery was interrupted by adversity and resistance. It must have been quite discouraging to face so much ongoing opposition. The reality is that when we set out to do something for God we anticipate a certain level of resistance and opposition. However, for all of us there is a breaking point or the feeling that enough is enough.

Right before we are at our breaking point is often when we find the enemy working the hardest. Isaac and his men must have been weary of digging and dealing with disappointment. They must have been tired and wishing or hoping for some type of breakthrough. Then it happened. They discovered Rehoboth and there was no strife. They found water and faced no adversity. There was no quarreling or bickering. Finally, they had found something which they could take as theirs and not be concerned with any opposition or resistance from the enemy.

Yet it was at Rehoboth where the enemy was working the hardest.

We must realize and understand that the enemy of our souls is crafty and sly. Peter declares that he is "looking for someone to devour" (1 Peter 5:8). When he recognizes that we are at the point of breaking or giving up one might think he would pick up the attack and resistance. However, what Rehoboth represents, a wide, roomy or comfortable place in

72

which to settle, is most often his tactic. We find ourselves in such a place with no visible opposition and we believe we have arrived at the perfect or ultimate destination.

God had blessed Isaac with water at Esek and opposition arose. God had blessed Isaac with water at Sitnah and adversity ensued. God blessed Isaac with water at Rehoboth and crickets chirp. What would you or I think or believe in that moment? I do not know about you, but my response would be, "Woohoo! Praise God, we have arrived!" That was Isaac's response as well. The greatest deception or attack the enemy levied on Isaac and his men was not strife or adversity, but rather a place of comfort and relief at the expense of peace and the presence of God.

Isaac had begun to prosper and to be blessed in great ways by God. The Philistines were not happy about this and they had covered over the wells. This was a direct act of war and a tactic of intimidation. The Philistines did not want Isaac to realize the fullness of God in, on, for or through his life. As Isaac was digging and opening the wells it caused the enemy to react defensively. The enemy's desire was to stop the forward movement of God's people.

Think about this for a moment. What his father had made available to Isaac had been covered over by the enemy. And the enemy was confident that Isaac would move on or forget about the wells and not risk stirring up the adversary or facing any warfare from him. Satan is a master intimidator and acts boldly in hopes of causing you and me to cower and retreat. Then, when someone takes the approach of Isaac and begins to take back what the enemy has stolen, he goes on the defensive and tries to stop God's children from faithfully seeing things through to the end.

Strife, contention, quarreling, adversity, and things of this nature do not just happen. These are the tools and the tricks of our enemy, things used with the intention of distorting our perspective. If our perspective becomes distorted we become quite susceptible to becoming deceived. And you always find destruction on the heels of deception. When you press beyond the intimidation and begin to lay claim to what your Father has made available to you, the enemy will work hard to bring you to your end result, destruction.

If that which is hard does not stop you in your tracks, Satan will try to deceive you with that which is easy and comfortable. Again, relief is not the same as peace.

As mentioned before, Rehoboth is marked by extensive ruins. It gave the appearance of a great place to settle, but in reality, it consumed those who chose to settle there. Just because something appears to be a blessing or favorable does not automatically mean it truly is. Consider this information taken directly from an online bible study.[11]

Rehoboth is one of the wells dug by Isaac (Genesis 26:22). 8 hours Southwest of Beersheba. "Once this must have been a city of not less than 12,000 or 15,000 inhabitants. Now it is a perfect field of ruins, a scene of unutterable desolation, across which the passing stranger can with difficulty, find his way." Huntington (Palestine and Its Transformation, 124) describes considerable remains of a suburban population extending both to the North and to the South of this once important place.
E. W. G. Masterman

The description is almost breathtaking. "Now it is a perfect field of ruins, a scene of unutterable desolation, across which the passing stranger can with difficulty, find his way."

---

[11] Biblestudytools.com

Imagine the glee of the enemy as he considers his work. Those who had taken the bait and settled at Rehoboth had found themselves quietly spiraling toward unutterable desolation. The painted picture of blessing and life turned into a life lesson of deception and death.

It is also important to note that Rehoboth is described as being "8 hours Southwest of Beersheba." This is significant in that the final place to where Isaac moved and dug was Beersheba. As we will see later in the story and in this book, Beersheba was the place where Isaac encountered God's presence and came to know Him as His own God, not just as the God of his father Abraham. Beersheba was the place that God was ultimately taking Isaac and it was such a short distance from Rehoboth. It did not even represent a full day's journey, even in the days of Isaac. There is such an important lesson for us in this geographical fact.

We often find ourselves stopping just short of God's ultimate place of blessing and breakthrough.

I am reminded of a story I once heard about a family who had poured all the money they had into some property in Colorado, buying some heavy mining equipment to mine the property in search of precious metal. The family worked tirelessly for days and months but continuously came up empty handed. Finally, the husband had reached his breaking point and decided to sell the land and the equipment to someone for mere pennies on the dollar. The family walked away with financial loss and emotional scars. As the story goes, the new owner of the land and equipment discovered a large and lucrative amount of silver after only thirty minutes of mining. The original family had given up hope and missed out on their reward by such a small margin.

What if Isaac had decided to settle and stay at Rehoboth? What if the feeling of relief and the end of the strife and adversity had lured him into a comfort zone mentality? What if he and his men had determined that Rehoboth was good enough? I cannot help but wonder how history may have turned out differently had Isaac not continued to dig and pursue God's purpose and God's best.

What about you? Are you teetering on the brink of settling in your Rehoboth? What is it that would potentially be lost or sacrificed if you stopped digging and settled for what is comfortable and providing relief? My prayer through this book is that both you and I would, just keep digging. I want all of us to discover the fullness of what God has, that which is found in the place of His presence.

You will make known to me the path of life; in Your presence is fullness of joy; in Your right hand there are pleasures forever.
Psalm 16:11

Chapter 8: Can I Dig Again?

How hard is it to move from Rehoboth? What type of resolve does it take to continue digging and pressing in when it seems that you have arrived at a special or blessed place? Genesis 26 says, *from there he went up to Beersheba.* The wording "went up" gives the picture of effort being needed to get where you are going. It speaks of climbing and working against what is natural, rather than having what seems natural working in your favor. Consider Isaiah's prophetic look at the last days:

Now it will come about that in the last days the mountain of the house of the Lord will be established as the chief of the mountains, and will be raised above the hills; and all the nations will stream to it. And many peoples will come and say, "Come, let us go up to the mountain of the Lord, to the house of the God of Jacob; that He may teach us concerning His ways and that we may walk in His paths."
Isaiah 2:2-3

The image painted is that of "going up" to meet with the Lord. It is the same image painted of Moses "going up" to Mount Sinai to meet with the Lord, while leading the children of Israel out of bondage and toward the Promised Land. It is also the same image of Jesus taking Peter, James and John up on the mountain of transfiguration where they were met with a glorified version of Christ and heard the voice of the Lord. The message that seems to resonate throughout Scripture is that of God calling us to a higher place with Him, a higher place *in* Him.

I do not want to over-analyze or draw false conclusions, but we often find that the pursuit of what God has for us in an uphill climb. As we alluded to in Chapter Seven, easy does

77

not automatically equal right. I am not saying that if something comes easy it is automatically not good. We do have to discern and understand, however, if what has come easy is really worth having in our lives.

Testing of D.I.G.

Continuing to dig and move beyond Rehoboth was not an easy decision. Let's revisit information from Chapter Two where we discussed what it means to D.I.G. - the acronym was Desire, Intent and Guts. According to dictionary.com the following definitions and synonyms are provided. [12]

Desire = want or longing; synonyms: ambition, appetite, aspiration, attraction, craving, devotion, eagerness, hunger, inclination, passion, urge or will.

Intent = determined or resolute; synonyms: alert, attending, bent, bound, committed, concentrated, decided, earnest, firm, fixed, focused, immersed, resolved, steadfast.

Guts = nerve or boldness; synonyms: audacity, backbone, courage, fortitude, grit, heart, patience, spine, spirit or spunk.

Each of these elements was put to the test for Isaac and his men after they discovered the well of Rehoboth. Considering how easy it would have been to settle, and even how common it was for others to settle, he had to make a bold determination to keep digging. It was vitally important for him to count the cost at that moment, to decide whether or not the next unknown step of the journey was worth giving up this new-found comfortable place.

The glaring question before Isaac and his men was whether or not anything could be better than Rehoboth. They

---

[12] Dictionary.com

had to determine if this was the destination. Often that is true with us as well. We find ourselves in our Rehoboth and we must determine whether this place of relief and comfort is our final destination. If we move on, will we be able to find anything better than Rehoboth?

Was the **desire** still there? Had the strife, contention and adversity curbed Isaac's appetite? At the beginning of the journey, he was convinced of that for which he was searching. Along the way, as we have discovered, there was quite a lot of resistance, trial and opposition. Rehoboth offered a logical alternative. While it was not *the* destination it was *a* destination – and even a comfortable and seemingly favorable one. It is so easy for our passion and will to press in, press on and press through to be stolen away by the battles that arise as a result of our digging.

Aside from this story about Isaac continuing to dig the wells, my favorite biblical account of desire overriding difficulty is found in Judges and the recounting of Gideon and his 300 warriors. Gideon had just led the small army to a miraculous victory. They had been marching and pursuing God's best at a pace and with an intensity rarely seen. And nestled in Judges 8 we find this fascinating statement:

*Then Gideon and the 300 men who were with him came to the Jordan and crossed over, **weary yet pursuing**.*
Judges 8:4

Gideon and his men had just completed a major battle in which God wrought a miraculous victory by their hand. Despite their fatigue they were not finished with all that God had called and commissioned them to accomplish. And we find them still in pursuit of their purpose, not allowing themselves to be hindered by weariness or fatigue.

Both with Isaac and with Gideon we find that difficulty and weariness do not have to stop our pursuit. Desire and the fire of that desire can continue to burn regardless of the circumstances we encounter. Paul told the Galatians to not become weary in well doing, because if they would not give up, they would reap (see Galatians 6:9).

What about **intent**? Was the intent of Isaac and his men still the same? The enemy had been trying very hard to steal away their focus and commitment. If the enemy can convince us to quit or give in he can get us to a place of defeat. I recently saw an illustration of a man who was underground with a pick axe walking away from his digging efforts. The implication was that he had grown weary and was giving up on his pursuit. Little did he know that he was inches away from the breakthrough he had spent so much time pursuing.

Hear these words again:

If you are slack in the day of distress, your strength is limited.
Proverb 24:10

When situations become difficult the ones who back down lack strength, ability, or efficiency. The reason people succumb to this is not that their intentions are wrong. The primary reason we find failed or incomplete intention or focus is that we often get our eyes in the wrong place. I believe wholeheartedly the reason Isaac was able to stay fixed upon the purpose of digging the wells was that he kept his heart fixed upon his pursuit of God. An elementary yet powerful thing to keep in mind is this:

Our own strength will always be small. It is in and through the strength of God that we endure. If we rely on ourselves, we will be prone to giving up in the midst of difficulty. Yet our reliance upon Him and His strength produces endurance and victory.

In Mark 10 we find what I consider to be the greatest example of focused intent recorded in Scripture. Jesus is on His way to Jerusalem where He knows He is going to be betrayed, beaten and brutally killed. Yet it does not slow His pursuit or purpose. It was for this reason He had come into the world and He was intent upon fulfilling that purpose. Look at the words Mark uses to paint this picture:

And they were in the way going up to Jerusalem; and Jesus went before them: and they were amazed; and as they followed, they were afraid. And he took again the twelve, and began to tell them what things should happen unto him.
Mark 10:32 (KJV)

As Jesus and His disciples were on their way to Jerusalem, Jesus was out in front leading the way with so much resolve that it both amazed and frightened the disciples. This was serious. The disciples saw first-hand the level of focus Jesus had in completing His task. It is easy to be on board with or excited about the vision and resolve of someone else, until you realize he is completely dedicated and serious in their pursuit and their mission. We find as the story plays out that the disciples fled and scattered after Jesus was arrested. In reality Jesus was trying desperately to impart to them both the intent and the importance of the intent necessary for the destination toward which they were moving.

I imagine that the men with Isaac had to deal with similar feelings. I picture Isaac being so focused and intent on finding the well of promise that it was as if he had tunnel vision. I cannot help but wonder if the others tried to convince him it was futile to continue and that they should consider moving on and cutting their losses.

Then we have **guts** or nerve. Would Isaac continue to show the backbone needed to keep on the journey toward discovering God's place of promise, blessing and presence?

Consider this account of the voyage of the Mayflower in 1620 as shared on sermoncentral.com by Pastor Steve Malone[13]:

On Sept 16, 1620 2 ships set sail from Plymouth England, The Speedwell and the Mayflower. The Speedwell encountered much difficulty as they began their journey springing many leaks in the ship. So when the 2 ships went to Port in Plymouth England, the Speedwell decided to go no further and 42 passengers from the Speedwell joined the 60 passengers and 30 crew members aboard the Mayflower.

Of the 102 passengers on board the Mayflower the majority were devout Christians. They were coming to America to shake loose from the bonds of the Church of England so they could worship God as they believed scriptures taught. And with great excitement and expectations that set sail for a new land... It wasn't long before the trip became difficult for several reasons, as noted by William Bradford an historian on the Mayflower, who would later become Governor of the colony for 33 years. Many of the passengers became sea sick as huge waves would crash over the deck of the ship... The nights were cold, damp and dark... Remember there was no indoor plumbing or electricity. And to make matters worse one of the crew, a very large man would constantly curse and

---

[13] Sermoncentral.com

abuse those who were sick... saying he was going to throw them overboard and steal all of their possessions.

They encountered many fierce storms which shook the ship with tremendous force. So fierce that many times they could not even keep the sail out and the force of the wind -- eventually cracked and bowed the main beams when they had just went over the half-way point across the Atlantic. And although the passengers and crew wanted to turn back, Christopher Jones, the ships Master, assured all that the vessel was "strong and firm under water." He ordered the beam to be secured. It was hoisted into place by a great iron screw that, fortunately, the Pilgrims brought out of Holland. AND Upon raising the beam, they "committed themselves to the will of God and resolved to proceed." These 100 people; cold, wet -- on wooden ship in the middle of the ocean -- put their hope, trust and lives into the hands of God. The battered ship finally came within sight of Cape Cod on November 19, 1620. Two had died at sea and two had given birth. The Pilgrims scanned the shoreline just to the west of them and described it as, "a goodly land wooded to the brink of the sea," William Bradford writes, "After long beatings at sea they fell with that land which is called Cape Cod and they were not a little joyful . . ."

The journey was tumultuous but the journey was worth it. As mentioned before, when you are going to the right place the destination will pay the price of the journey. Along the way it takes guts and fortitude to not give up but to continue in the pursuit.

It takes a great deal of courage to pursue God's purpose. I know there are some who brazenly declare that Christianity is nothing more than a crutch for the weak. However nothing could be further from the truth. Christianity and the journey with God are neither for the faint of heart nor for the weak. Christianity is the ultimate badge of courage.

During the journey from Gerar to Beersheba, Isaac and his men encountered many setbacks along the way. Yet deep inside them was the desire, intent, and guts to just keep digging. In the next and final section of this book, we will discover the reward they received as a result of their determination.

Section 5: Beersheba

From there he went up to Beersheba. That night the Lord appeared to him and said, "I am the God of your father Abraham. Do not be afraid, for I am with you; I will bless you and will increase the number of your descendants for the sake of my servant Abraham." Isaac built an altar there and called on the name of the Lord. There he pitched his tent, and there his servants dug a well.

Now it came about on the same day, that Isaac's servants came in and told him about the well which they had dug, and said to him, "We have found water." So he called it Shibah; therefore the name of the city is Beersheba to this day.
Genesis 26:23-25, 32-33

Beersheba is the well of seven or water of an oath.

In Genesis 21, Abraham covenanted with Abimelech about this well for the price of seven lambs.

Beersheba is the place where God appeared to Isaac.

Chapter 9: The Place of Covenant

In Genesis 21 we find the story of Abraham and Abimelech. Abimelech recognized that there was something different about Abraham and declared about Abraham, *"God is with you in all that you do" (Genesis 21:22).* It was obvious to Abimelech that Abraham had the favor of God upon his life. Yet even within that recognition there was a problem that arose regarding a well of water.

*But Abraham complained to Abimelech because of **the well of water which the servants of Abimelech had seized.** And Abimelech said, "I do not know who has done this thing; you did not tell me, nor did I hear of it until today."*
Genesis 21:25-26

We find here that the well in Beersheba had been dug by Abraham, and the men and servants of Abimelech had taken it away in a violent manner. This is the well to which God was ultimately bringing Isaac in order for Isaac to encounter Him in a real and personal way. The very place of blessing that had been opened and discovered by Abraham – a representative of the Father – was immediately stolen away by the servants of Abimelech.

Abimelech means "my father is king," and he was the king of Gerar. In Section One we defined Gerar as lodging or holding place. Further study shows the root garar means "to drag or to drag away." Proverb 21:7 declares that the violence of the wicked will drag him away. Therefore, let us see Abimelech as meaning his father is the king of that which drags away.

The picture is that of the enemy seeking to steal, kill, and destroy anything good that God has given to His people.

As we have considered through the first three wells, Satan will use strife, adversity, or even false comfort and peace to try and keep us from taking hold of God's best. Abimelech was not a bad person, he simply served as a shadow or type of how Satan will work to take away God's blessing.

Let us recall that the journey of Isaac and his men toward Beersheba began in the valley of Gerar. When they began to dig and discovered Esek, they were confronted and challenged by the men of Gerar. They had their discovery taken away from them. The full-circle picture is that the enemy is ultimately trying to intimidate us to the point of giving up and failing to realize or embrace that which truly belongs to us. Yet something very fascinating takes place after Isaac moves on to Beersheba. I want to focus on this to gain an understanding concerning the place of covenant to which God was bringing Isaac.

Then Abimelech came to him from Gerar with his adviser Ahuzzath and Phicol the commander of his army. Isaac said to them, "Why have you come to me, since you hate me and have sent me away from you?" They said, "We see plainly that the Lord has been with you; so we said, 'Let there now be an oath between us, even between you and us, and let us make a covenant with you, that you will do us no harm, just as we have not touched you and have done to you nothing but good and have sent you away in peace. You are now the blessed of the Lord.'" Then he made them a feast, and they ate and drank. In the morning they arose early and exchanged oaths; then Isaac sent them away and they departed from him in peace.
Genesis 26:26-31

When Isaac and his men arrived in Beersheba, the place of the covenant, Abimelech and his men came quickly to him to make peace and to renew the covenant that he had made with Abraham. Is it not intriguing that the same ones who as Isaac says, "Hate (him) and have sent (him) away from (them)," come to offer peace and even to seek mercy? Can I tell you that the last thing the enemy wants a child of God to do is to come to the place of covenant or fulfillment to which God has called them and to which He desires to take them. All along it was the desire of the enemy to keep Isaac from realizing the fullness of the promise and potential, but now that he had moved to Beersheba it was obvious there was no stopping him.

There is a place in Christ that is available to each and every one of us and the enemy is fighting hard to prevent our arrival. The Psalmist declares that *he who dwells in the shelter of the Most High will abide in the shadow of the Almighty (Psalm 91:1).*

God is looking to bring us beyond the strife, the adversity, the false sense of security and peace and into that place of covenant rest with Him. Yes there are trials and challenges along the way and on the journey. Yes there are times when striving and facing battles, storms and challenges is a necessary part. However, what God intends is for us to come to the place in Him where everything around us pales in comparison to the *peace that passes understanding (see Philippians 4:7)* that we find and enjoy only in relationship with Him.

Beersheba in the Beginning

Let us go back to Genesis 21 and the beginning of the place of covenant.

Abraham took sheep and oxen and gave them to Abimelech, and the two of them made a covenant. Then Abraham set

*seven ewe lambs of the flock by themselves. Abimelech said
to Abraham, "What do these seven ewe lambs mean, which
you have set by themselves?" He said, **"You shall take
these seven ewe lambs from my hand so that it may be
a witness to me, that I dug this well."** Therefore he called
that place Beersheba, because there the two of them took an
oath. So they made a covenant at Beersheba; and Abimelech
and Phicol, the commander of his army, arose and returned to
the land of the Philistines. Abraham planted a tamarisk tree at
Beersheba, and there he called on the name of the Lord,
the Everlasting God. And Abraham sojourned in the land of
the Philistines for many days.
Genesis 21:27-34*

Beersheba speaks of an oath, an agreement or an understanding. When the covenant agreement was made by Abraham and Abimelech, it came with the understanding that within that place there would be peace. We understand from Scripture that Abraham was blessed by God and those he encountered did not always roll out the red carpet for him. There was some intimidation. There was some jealousy. There was a sense of territorialism. Nobody was interested in simply giving everything over to Abraham.

We find that Beersheba was essentially purchased by Abraham. He saw such importance in the well of water and the significance of Beersheba that it was worth the price of the seven ewe lambs and the covenant entered into with Abimelech. These men entered into an agreement that at Beersheba there would be the understanding that the well and the place belonged to Abraham and his seed. Whereas the places along the journey brought about much strife and contention, at Beersheba there was peace and cessation from battle.

Christom is the Purchaser of Spiritual Beersheba

Christ is the Purchaser of Spiritual Beersheba

God wants us to understand that He has prepared for us a place in Him that is a place of peace and cessation from battle. That place in Him has been prepared because, like Beersheba, it has been purchased by the Father through One Lamb – Jesus Christ.

Galatians 3 goes into great detail concerning our place in Christ and our position as heirs of the promise and of the covenant as related to Abraham. The covenant at Beersheba serves as a type, therefore, of the greater covenant God has established with Abraham for all of those who are in Christ. In the same way in which Isaac realized freedom, blessing and favor at Beersheba, so too do we, as believers, realize freedom, blessing and favor in Christ.

Even so Abraham believed God, and it was reckoned to him as righteousness. Therefore, be sure that it is those who are of faith who are sons of Abraham….So then those who are of faith are blessed with Abraham, the believer….Christ redeemed us from the curse of the Law, having become a curse for us – for it is written, "Cursed is everyone who hangs on a tree" – in order that in Christ Jesus the blessing of Abraham might come to the Gentiles, so that we would receive the promise of the Spirit through faith….And if you belong to Christ, then you are Abraham's descendants, heirs according to promise.
Galatians 3:6-7, 9, 13-14, 29

Because of the work of Christ – the Lamb slain before the foundation of the earth – we can come into the spiritual Beersheba, and enjoy the fullness of God and the power of His Spirit without strife. We can abide in Him and find ourselves lacking nothing. We can come to that place of life, joy and peace in the Spirit. That is the destination. That is why we just keep digging.

So many times we find ourselves quitting or stopping short of that place in Him. Even now I am struggling to articulate what I want to say, as I fail to understand all that God has made available to me.

When Isaac and his men arrived in Beersheba they encountered a favor with the enemy that heretofore had not been realized. They stepped into the place that had been purchased by father Abraham, the place of covenant. When Isaac and his men arrived at Beersheba, the enemy recognized they were unable to do anything in opposition at the place of covenant, and Abimelech recognized the favor of God upon Isaac.

God desires that His people experience and walk in His favor. Favor is defined as "the state of being approved or held in regard."[14] To be in God's favor means that you have His approval on your life. It is like having His smile upon you and having His blessing accompany all that you do. God's favor is available for anyone who commits his ways to Him and pursues that place in Him.

Isaac did not have favor at Esek, but there he dealt with strife and contention. He did not suddenly find himself favored in Sitnah, but there he experienced adversity and all hell breaking loose. At first it seemed Rehoboth was a place of favor, but in reality it was a deceptive place of comfort. The favor and secret place for Isaac was found in Beersheba because it was the place of covenant.

---

[14] Dictionary.com

Rather than spending our time and spinning our wheels racing toward false finish lines we should dig and move until we position ourselves in that place of favor and blessing in Christ that the enemy does not have access to because it has been purchased by the precious blood of the Lamb. From Gerar through Rehoboth there were problems, because they all ultimately represented territory to which the enemy still had access. Yet, Beersheba represents a demilitarized zone in that the battle has been won and paid in full.

Chapter 10: The Place of Remembrance

Not only was Beersheba the place of covenant, but for Isaac there was a level of familiarity with Beersheba. It was the place he remembered. The Introduction of this book opens with this paragraph:

The sound of the ram in the thicket must have been a wonderful and welcome sound for Isaac, as he looked up at his father Abraham, who stood with his slaying knife aimed at his son (see Genesis 22). Isaac was the promised son born to Abraham and Sarah, and God had challenged Abraham to offer him as a sacrifice. Isaac got to see first-hand the faith of his father in a way that few others have been able to experience.

In some ways this seems out of place with the message of this book; but in this chapter we will connect these stories and see how they play a prominent role in finding Beersheba – the place to which God is taking us. As father and son were making their way up the mountain for Abraham to offer Isaac as a sacrifice to the Lord, a myriad of thoughts must have been running through both of their minds. Yet, in Abraham's heart, there was a knowing that God was going to provide.

There is something of significance, however, concerning what Abraham did after God provided the sacrifice in place of Isaac. It is important for us to note:

So Abraham returned to his young men, and they arose and went together to Beersheba; and Abraham lived at Beersheba.
Genesis 22:19

Following his willingness to sacrifice Isaac and seeing God provide, Abraham went to and lived at Beersheba. We know from Genesis 21 that Abraham sojourned in the land of the Philistines many days. Yet we see here that after experiencing a mighty provision from God, the place in which he chose to dwell was Beersheba. Abraham chose to dwell in the place of covenant.

The Bible is unclear as to Isaac's age at the time of God's call for Abraham to offer him as a sacrifice. There are some clues surrounding the possible age in the life-span of his mother Sarah, the conversation they had on the way up the mountain and the carrying of the wood as he journeyed. This information has led many scholars to believe Isaac to be in his late teens or early twenties when the sacrifice was requested by God. We know that Isaac would have been thirty-seven years old at the time of his mother's death, and so we can assume that he would have potentially spent fifteen to twenty years in Beersheba after the provision of God.

Therefore, when Isaac arrived at Beersheba in Genesis 26 he would have felt at home. It would have been a familiar place for him. What I am about to say may very well be the most important statement of this entire book; please do not miss it.

The reason Isaac did not stop at any point in the journey is because he knew from experience the value of Beersheba.

When you do not know the value of the place to which you are going, it can be very easy to get sidetracked and to stop at various points along the way. It would seem apparent that, having spent time in Beersheba before, Isaac knew and understood the value of getting back again.

In Genesis 24 when Isaac took Rebekah as his wife, he was living in the Negev or in the south country of the land of Judah (Genesis 24:62). Geographically, this is located in the general vicinity of Gerar and the region in which Isaac began the process of digging the wells. Yet it is also representative of a distance from Beersheba. Then a famine arose some time later and caused him to begin to move toward Beersheba.

I imagine that as Isaac moved toward Gerar there was something inside of him that began to reminisce and to remember the good things of and from Beersheba. Those memories, along with the emotions stirred by those memories, began to drive him to dig and find or rediscover the place he knew.

Enough time had passed for Isaac's sons to be born and for Esau to sell his birthright to Jacob for a bowl of stew. Life had moved on and situations had arisen that in some ways made Beersheba seem like a distant memory at best. Nonetheless, as he got closer to Beersheba, there was a reconnecting and a drive from deep within him that was unwilling to stop until he had arrived at the place which he remembered from his youth.

Isaac dug the wells and went in pursuit of Beersheba because he was longing to get back to that which he had known and experienced in the earlier years of his life. There was something about the place of covenant that continuously drew him back. I get the feeling that he sensed lack and disappointment in every place he had found himself since leaving Beersheba, and he was going to do whatever it took to get back there again.

Do You Remember?

Do you have that place as well? I am not talking geographically or a look back to your formative childhood years. There will always be a sense of nostalgia when one considers their hometown. I recall so many things from growing up in a small town in Indiana. Many things in life bring me back to my days at 602 South Holland Street, but that is not the place of remembrance to which I am referring.

What about that secret place with God? What about that spiritual place where you walked in the blessing and favor of God? Are you there now? If not, do you long to return and dwell there again? Can you remember and reflect on your own Beersheba – the place purchased for you by the Lamb of God, where you enjoyed all things God and all things good? Are you willing to dig and to do whatever is necessary to get back to that place?

Some of you reading this book are in Gerar. You are in a valley in your life and it feels that if you reached up as high as you can, you could almost touch bottom. I know that feeling. No matter how hard you try, you simply cannot figure out why you are at the place in which you find yourself, or what you could possibly do to get out. Isaac found himself in the valley of Gerar simply because it was along the path of the journey he was taking.

The same is true so often in our lives. Instead of trying to figure out what happened to get us to the valleys in our lives, it would be better for us to simply realize that these places are nothing more than part of the journey. Do we have the desire, intent and guts to keep digging until we get beyond that place, and one step closer to Beersheba?

Perhaps you are on such a journey in your life. You have moved on from the valley and you have encountered an Esek, a place of strife and contention. Perhaps that strife and contention has come from within your heart or even from those closest to you, and you are not sure if it is worth continuing on at all. Do you have the desire, intent and guts to keep digging until you get beyond that place, and one step closer to Beersheba?

Or maybe someone reading this book is in Sitnah. Maybe it seems that everywhere you turn you come face to face with the devil himself and the adversity which accompanies him. Perhaps right now you are wondering why it seems that you cannot catch a break to save your life, and you are considering whether or not anything is ever going to go your way. Do you have the desire, intent and guts to keep digging until you get beyond that place, and one step closer to Beersheba?

For the one who is in Rehoboth, feeling that you have finally arrived, there is a sense of comfort and relief – this is a dangerous place. Are you willing to keep going or is "good enough" going to be good enough for you? As we previously discussed, this can be the most dangerous place in which to find oneself. The danger of Rehoboth is the deception it can bring. It offers room and comfort, and even has deep wells as you find in Beersheba. Yet it is the place where more damage and ruins have taken place than anywhere else before this point.

In Rehoboth you finally feel that hell is not fighting against you; you struggle to know whether this is your destination or just a temporary rest area. Do you have the desire, intent and guts to keep digging until you get beyond that place and one step closer to Beersheba?

I believe the words of the Psalmist best sum this up when he says:

*I shall remember the deeds of the Lord; surely I will remember
your wonders of old. I will meditate on all Your work and
muse on Your deeds. Your way, O God, is holy; what god is
great like our God? You are the God who works wonders;
You have made known Your strength among the peoples.
You have by Your power redeemed Your people, the sons of
Jacob and Joseph.
Psalm 77:11-15*

There have been times in my life where I have felt defeated, helpless and hopeless. I have wanted to crawl under a rock or simply hide in a secluded place. It seemed in those moments as if nothing was going right and there was no end in sight to the difficulty I was facing. But in those times I found there was strength and resolve that came from remembering the goodness of God, and remembering the good places that God has taken me in my life. I may not in that moment feel or believe that I am in a good place, but I can call to remembrance the blessing and favor of God in my Beersheba. This will stir in my heart and spirit a resolve to dig and press on to get back to that place once again.

In another place the Psalmist encourages us to *taste and see that the Lord is good (Psalm 34:8)*. When we have tasted that which is good, we find ourselves intent to get back to that place no matter the cost. Isaac had that connection with Beersheba. To him it was the only destination. Regardless of what any spiritual or natural enemy tried to throw at him to stop him, he was going to just keep digging to get back to Beersheba. Isaac was determined to get back to the place he remembered, because he knew the destination was worth the price of the journey.

Chapter 11: The Place of His Presence

From there he went up to Beersheba. That night the Lord appeared to him and said, "I am the God of your father Abraham. Do not be afraid, for I am with you; I will bless you and will increase the number of your descendants for the sake of my servant Abraham." Isaac built an altar there and called on the name of the Lord. There he pitched his tent, and there his servants dug a well.
Genesis 26:23-25

The very first thing that happened when Isaac "went up to Beersheba" was that the Lord appeared to him. In this, I see the Lord responding to his persistence and desire to get back to Beersheba. It is important to note that Isaac encountered God at Beersheba before he even dug the well. Note this:

In the previous locations Isaac dug a well and discovered what the place had to offer. In Beersheba, however, he dug a well after he realized it was the place where he encountered God.

The valuable lesson is that when we dig and search in our own strength we find that which can be produced in natural ways. Yet when we discover God's presence, we find that is the place of blessing and the place of His presence, where we find the waters worth finding. The Psalmist declares that fullness of joy is found in the Lord's presence (Psalm 16:11).

We can understand that we are on the right track when we encounter opposition from the enemy. We can know we have reached our destination when we encounter the presence of the Lord. Ultimately that will be realized in

Heaven. Yet even here on earth, we can find that Beersheba place in Him, that place where we enjoy His presence and all of the blessings that accompany His presence.

His Presence Trumps All Things

I once went through a time of Bible study on the differences between the anointing, the gifts of God and the presence of God. Some of what I discovered I shared with our church during a sermon. As I have pondered these important elements of Scripture and the nature of God I find there is an overwhelming conclusion to which I have come: I want the presence of God more than I want anointing or gifting.

What I have realized is that you can have the anointing without the presence. Ezekiel speaks of the King of Tyre, a passage often used in reference to Lucifer, as the "anointed cherub" (Ezekiel 28). From this reference, one can draw a conclusive understanding that Lucifer was *the anointed cherub,"* but his actions showed that he clearly did not have the presence of God at work or as a priority in his heart. Ezekiel declares that *"you were blameless . . . until unrighteousness was found in you."*

Also, you can have the gifts of God without His presence. Jesus declared that many on the last day will declare they have operated in the gifts, but He will tell them to depart for they did not know Him (Matthew 7:22-24). Even though they flowed in the gifts, their end shows they chose the gifts above the presence of God.

When Isaac found God's presence he knew he was home. He immediately responded by building an altar and then his men dug a well. There is within all of us an ability to recognize and feel at home in the presence of God. The problem occurs when anointing and gifting take precedence over His presence.

Samson serves as a perfect biblical example of this sad reality. Time after time Delilah asked him to reveal to her the source of his great strength. Time after time he told her a lie, but a study of the story reveals that each lie was closer to the truth. Ultimately Samson disclosed his secret. Delilah cut off his hair and called the Philistines to come and attack Samson. When the Philistines came he got up to fight them as he had always done, and the Bible says *"he did not know that the Lord had departed from him" (Judges 16:20)*. Samson was anointed and gifted by God, but he did not value the presence of God.

More than anything else, I desire that we would all long for His presence to the point that nothing else will be able to satisfy. I want each of us to come to the place that says when strife, opposition, adversity, or apparent relief arise we refuse to stop but choose rather to continue on until we encounter the presence of God Himself.

His Presence Makes it Personal

For Isaac it was not just about being Abraham's son any longer. When God appeared to him at Beersheba He declared, *"I am the God of your father Abraham. Do not be afraid, for I am with you; I will bless you and will increase the number of your descendants for the sake of my servant Abraham."* God was letting Isaac know without question Whom he was encountering. At the same time God was letting Isaac know that He was his God as well.

Consider how that must have been for Isaac. He was the promised son of Abraham. Think about when he was playing with the other kids and they would not stop asking about his daddy. Or how many times did he hear whispers about Abraham and how awesome he was? Did he ever wonder if he could possibly be more than the son of Abraham? In this moment at Beersheba, God erased the doubts and answered the questions by declaring He was indeed the God of Isaac.

Have you struggled with similar doubts or questions? Does it sometimes feel you are caught in the shadows cast by someone else and all you want is to be who God has made you to be?

There is a statement I have heard many times that I have found to be true. God does not have grandchildren, He only has children. In God's eyes each and every one of us is special; we are fearfully and wonderfully made. Many times the word of God to Jeremiah has resounded in my own heart and spirit.

"Before I formed you in the womb I knew you, and before you were born I consecrated you; I have appointed you a prophet to the nations."
Jeremiah 1:5

God declared to Isaac that He was the God of Isaac in the same way in which He had always been known as the God of Abraham. That is the beauty of the presence of the Lord. He comes near and makes it personal and real for each of us.

His Presence Brings Completion

Isaac's men informed him they had found water in the well in Beersheba. Isaac called the well Sibah. This is the only time we find this word used in the Scripture and it means "seven."

102

It is at once a look back at the covenant while also a look ahead to the promise. Abraham purchased Beersheba from Abimelech for seven ewe lambs, establishing a covenant between the two of them. Beersheba was a declaration to Isaac of the genuine peace, rest and blessing that can be found in God's presence. Beersheba represents a promise to us of God's ongoing covenant and all that He has made available in His presence.

The number seven has always represented completion and rest. God created the earth in six days, and He rested on the seventh day. So I hear Isaac making a declaration before God and to his men: "We have arrived. Our journey is complete. This is the place of rest. This is the place for which we have been searching." Through his father Abraham Beersheba had been purchased as the place of covenant. Now through his own tenacity he found himself back in that place once again.

The writer of Hebrews challenges us to *"be diligent to enter that rest"* (Hebrews 4:11). Friends, there is a completion and a rest that is found in His presence that will never be found in any other place. No matter how hard we search, and no matter where we search, aside from His presence, we will always come up void.

It is also important to note that following his encounter with the presence of God, Abimelech approached Isaac and referred to him as the blessed of the Lord (see Genesis 26:28). Isaac did not have to declare himself to be blessed. It was obvious that he was blessed. God's presence has a greater impact on the life of an individual than anything else.

Chapter 12: The Blessings of Beersheba

The well of Beersheba was known to be deep and plenteous. God's presence fits that very description. God's presence is deep and plenteous in and for our lives. There is no lack found in Him. And we know that in all things God will continue and perform what He began.

Beersheba was claimed by Abraham from Abimelech and it was the place of covenant. As we have outlined in this book, Beersheba was the place to which Isaac journeyed to find the place he remembered. It was in Beersheba that Isaac discovered the presence of God in and for his own life. But I find it interesting that the story of Beersheba does not end there. Before concluding this book I want to take a brief moment and look at the continued blessing and significance of Beersheba.

So Isaac called Jacob and blessed him and charged him, and said to him, "You shall not take a wife from the daughters of Canaan. Arise, go to Paddan-aram, to the house of Bethuel your mother's father; and from there take to yourself a wife from the daughters of Laban your mother's brother. May God Almighty bless you and make you fruitful and multiply you, that you may become a company of peoples. May He also give you the blessing of Abraham, to you and to your descendants with you, that you may possess the land of your sojournings, which God gave to Abraham." Then Isaac sent Jacob away, and he went to Paddan-aram to Laban, son of Bethuel the Aramean, the brother of Rebekah, the mother of Jacob and Esau....Then Jacob departed from Beersheba and went toward Haran.
Genesis 28:1-5, 10

When Isaac blessed his son Jacob to go and take for himself a wife, the blessing and sending took place in Beersheba. When Jacob departed from Isaac and Rebekah, he departed from Beersheba. The continuation of God's plan once again finds a connection with Beersheba – the place of covenant and the presence of God.

Years later we find Jacob having another encounter with God at Beersheba. When it became known to him that his son Joseph was in Egypt and that Jacob and his family was making their way to Egypt to reconnect with him, God met with Jacob in Beersheba.

So Israel set out with all that he had, and came to Beersheba, and offered sacrifices to the God of his father Isaac. God spoke to Israel in visions of the night and said, "Jacob, Jacob." And he said, "Here I am." He said, "I am God, the God of your father; do not be afraid to go down to Egypt, for I will make you a great nation there. I will go down with you to Egypt, and I will also surely bring you up again; and Joseph will close your eyes."
Genesis 46:1-4

Here we find Jacob having an encounter similar to that of his father Isaac. God appeared to him in Beersheba, renewing the covenant and making it personal with him. Beersheba carried significance with the three patriarchs of the faith – Abraham, Isaac and Jacob. For us the spiritual place of Beersheba carries significance with our faith. His presence establishes, confirms, and reaffirms our faith.

The final instance I want to consider is in 1 Kings 19. When Elijah fled from Jezebel afraid for his life, the Bible says he *"came to Beersheba, which belongs to Judah."* Elijah left his servant in Beersheba and moved on a bit further and

105

asked God to take his life. God met with him, encouraged him, and ultimately gave him instruction on what to do next in his life and ministry.

But what intrigues me beyond the Elijah connection is to whom the Bible says Beersheba belonged. During the division of the land, Beersheba became a possession of the tribe of Simeon (Joshua 19), which the Bible indicates was in the midst of the sons of Judah. It is believed that during the reign of King David, Beersheba was given back to the tribe of Judah. Therefore, in 1 Kings 19 we find that Beersheba is mentioned as belonging to Judah.

Why does this matter? Judah is the most well-known of the tribes of Israel, for it is the tribe from which we can trace the earthly lineage of Christ Himself (see the lineage of Christ as recorded in Matthew 1). Beersheba again points to significance of covenant, promise, faith and presence as found in the person of Jesus Christ. My favorite passage in reference to Christ and the tribe of Judah is in Revelation:

Then I began to weep greatly because no one was found worthy to open the book or to look into it; and one of the elders said to me, "Stop weeping; behold, the Lion that is from the tribe of Judah, the Root of David, has overcome so as to open the book and its seven seals."
Revelation 5:4-5

The blessing of Beersheba was never limited to one person. The blessing of a Beersheba place is still true today for all who find that secret place in Christ and His presence. May all of us at all times just keep digging to find and dwell at Beersheba.

Conclusion

And Isaac departed from there and camped in the valley of Gerar, and settled there. Then Isaac dug again the wells of water which had been dug in the days of his father Abraham, for the Philistines had stopped them up after the death of Abraham; and he gave them the same names which his father had given them. But when Isaac's servants dug in the valley and found there a well of flowing water, the herdsmen of Gerar quarreled with the herdsmen of Isaac, saying, "The water is ours!" So he named the well Esek, because they contended with him. Then they dug another well, and they quarreled over it too, so he named it Sitnah. He moved away from there and dug another well, and they did not quarrel over it; so he named it Rehoboth, for he said, "At last the Lord has made room for us, and we will be fruitful in the land." Then he went up from there to Beersheba. The Lord appeared to him the same night and said, "I am the God of your father Abraham; do not fear, for I am with you. I will bless you, and multiply your descendants, for the sake of My servant Abraham." So he built an altar there and called upon the name of the Lord, and pitched his tent there; and there Isaac's servants dug a well. Then Abimelech came to him from Gerar with his adviser Ahuzzath and Phicol the commander of his army. Isaac said to them, "Why have you come to me, since you hate me and have sent me away from you?" They said, "We see plainly that the Lord has been with you; so we said, 'Let there now be an oath between us, even between you and us, and let us make a covenant with you, that you will do us no harm, just as we have not touched you and have done to you nothing but good and have sent you away in peace. You are now the blessed of the Lord.'" Then he made them a feast, and they ate and drank. In the morning they arose early and exchanged oaths;

then Isaac sent them away and they departed from him in
peace. Now it came about on the same day, that Isaac's
servants came in and told him about the well which they had
dug, and said to him, "We have found water." So he called it
Shibah; therefore the name of the city is Beersheba to this
day.
Genesis 26:17-33

The herdsmen of Gerar quarreled with Isaac's men and said, "The water is ours!" Days later Abimelech, the king of Gerar, along with his adviser and army commander came to see Isaac in Beersheba. Here they declared to Isaac, "You are now the blessed of the Lord." The transition is a sharp contrast in opinion and approach. We see the move from the men of Gerar quarreling and fighting with Isaac, to the king of Gerar declaring Isaac to be blessed and asking him to join in a covenant of peace.

This transition to a new declaration was only made possible because Isaac and his men were willing to just keep digging until they arrived at Beersheba, renewing the covenant with God, and having a personal encounter with Him. Their faithful journey caused their enemies to recognize the blessing and favor of God that was upon their lives. No earthly enemy wants to find himself in a place of making that declaration. Neither does the enemy of our souls want to have to recognize anyone as the blessed of the Lord. Yet when we press in and dig to find God's presence, we put ourselves in the place where that is exactly what he must do.

In Acts 19, the seven sons of Sceva commanded an evil spirit to leave someone in the Name of Jesus whom Paul preaches. The demon spoke that he knew Jesus and he knew Paul, but he did not know the sons of Sceva. From this account we are reminded again that we can be known in Hell. Paul arrived at this place of recognition by the enemy in much the same was as did Isaac. He continued to dig and press to discover the fullness of the covenant relationship with Christ. I think Paul declared it best when he said,

Not that I have already obtained it or have already become perfect, but I press on so that I may lay hold of that for which also I was laid hold of by Christ Jesus. Brethren, I do not regard myself as having laid hold of it yet; but one thing I do: forgetting what lies behind and reaching forward to what lies ahead, I press on toward the goal for the prize of the upward call of God in Christ Jesus.
Philippians 3:12-14

There are times when digging and continuing to move forward can be the most difficult thing we can do. When the enemy brings strife and contention, there is a natural tendency in us to simply cut our losses and walk away. When we do go a little further, only to face adversity and Hell itself, it seems as though we are being ripped away from everything we thought we were pursuing. Then, at times, we find the enemy really getting crafty against us in that he allows us to feel a sense of comfort and relief that we mistake that for genuine peace.

All along the process and journey we find ample opportunity to quit. Nobody would probably blame us if we did, but there is a real blessing that comes with persevering and choosing to not give up no matter the cost. There is something supernatural that takes place when we decide to just keep digging. When we press through the challenges and battles, and we come to the destination of God's presence, we will find without a doubt that the destination pays the price of the journey. Finding Him in a personal way is worth anything it takes to get to that point.

I will conclude with the acronym D.I.G. once again. This sums up how we must continually respond to the journey from barrenness to blessing. If we faint and give up we may very well indeed miss out on the greatest thing available. As Paul says to the church in Galatia, *"Let us not lose heart in doing good, for in due time we will reap if we do not grow weary" (Galatians 6:9).* Therefore, let us . . .

1. Dig with DESIRE.

The first element to digging is **desire**. The picture is of wanting or longing for something to such an extent that you will do whatever it takes to possess it. Desire is that which takes root in your heart, and drives you to take possession of that which you desire. It was genuine desire that drove Isaac and his men to keep digging until they arrived at Beersheba.

2. Dig with INTENT.

The second element to digging is **intent**. It speaks of being so committed, so determined, so resolute that nothing is going to prevent you from reaching your desired end. Intentions that are genuine and properly placed will be found in those who accomplish great things. Because Isaac was intent on reaching Beersheba, there was nothing along the way that was going to hold him back.

3. Dig with GUTS.

The final element to digging is **guts.** This calls to mind the grit, backbone and even the patience required to accomplish your goal. Guts do not allow you to give up or give in, but to choose to press on and endure. At times a person with guts will find himself all alone, but a person with guts often finds himself on top. Because of the determination and guts of Isaac, they encountered God in a personal way in Beersheba.

There were many opportunities for Isaac to stop digging. When strife and contention arose over the waters of Esek, there was nothing keeping him from going back to Gerar or even to the Negev. Yet, he moved forward and kept digging. When adversity and great opposition surrounded the waters of Sitnah, it must have been tempting to retreat. Then, when they discovered the waters at Rehoboth and Isaac declared God had made room for them, they must have given serious consideration to putting down roots. The most likely place to settle is when things give the appearance of being easy or comfortable.

Nonetheless, through each step of this journey, Isaac and the men with him just kept digging. They did not allow circumstances to dictate their actions. They showed the resolve to rise above all things and dig until they discovered the blessing, favor and presence of God. My prayer is simple. May each of us go and do likewise. May each of us just keep digging.

Printed in Great Britain
by Amazon.co.uk, Ltd.,
Marston Gate.